ANDREI P. ... U

Life Dysmorphia

7 SCENTS OF LIFE: Time, Freedom, Happiness, Love, Succes, Wealth, Faith

Copyright © 2025 by Andrei P. Bălăceanu

All rights reserved. No part of this publication may be reproduced, stored or transmitted in any form or by any means, electronic, mechanical, photocopying, recording, scanning, or otherwise without written permission from the publisher. It is illegal to copy this book, post it to a website, or distribute it by any other means without permission.

First edition

This book was professionally typeset on Reedsy. Find out more at reedsy.com

Contents

1	Introduction	1
2	Time	22
3	Freedom	40
4	Happiness	53
5	Love	70
6	Success	83
7	Wealth	108
8	Faith	132
9	The flavor of life	151
10	The recipe of life	217

1

Introduction

Individual destiny, as a lived reality shaped by the discipline of being, freed from the compulsion to defame liberty, unfolds as if foreseen by a prophetic guide, one overly inspired, overly abstract, untethered from time and space. A singular, exceptional universe: the conscience. Around this inner cosmos revolve all principles, all preparation, all resolutions and revelations, all understanding of the external world.

Here, within the elevated realm of thought, the indecipherable is discerned, knowledge and experience intertwine; good clashes with evil, constancy with change. It is a space where anguish transforms into a problem, and hope emerges as a solution. It lies within each person's power to engage in battle according to their own capacity, but above all, it is imperative to embark upon the quest for meaning to rescue existence from the assault of nullity.

Some awaken to this truth too early, others too late, and a few never at all: that life is the beginning of a battle from which no one escapes, yet in the end, all are released with their final breath. Whether they will or not, all are inevitably taught the lessons of endurance. To grasp the necessity of struggle is to attain intelligence; to accept the peace that follows is to glimpse wisdom. Effort is the path along which we escort our existence, where we wrestle with confusion and deviation until direction is found, and with it, a life of dignity. The first and most profound reflex of existence, the primordial lesson life teaches, is the motion forward. Regardless of trials, traps, or despair, no one is permitted to linger forever in stagnation. The journey must be completed, unless one desires a premature ruin.

Into this ongoing confrontation enter, often obsessively, unseen forces, subtle spirits skilled in reshaping one's attitude. Beyond the struggle for existence, there are hidden encounters with the unfamiliar. It becomes essential to discern: who uplifts, and who diminishes; whom to shelter, and whom to cast out. The wise come to understand that within every human being reside both demons and angels. These are not mystical creatures, they are disciples of emotion. Not the other way around; they do not master, for the power of the master does not vanish with his absence, but with his isolation. Deprive him of disciples, and his influence wanes. Some spirits you may live with, others will undo you. The most insidious of all, the one that must be overcome without fail, is the demon that severs trust in oneself. Without self-trust, no aid is possible, not even divine.

And yet, not every fierce emotion must be extinguished, for to do so would be to exile all longing, all pleasure. Certain dark currents are needed, now and then, to intensify the sensation of being alive. Others must be subdued and awakened only at pivotal moments, especially when kindness turns traitor. Even a measure of cruelty has its place: to destroy the damaging innocence of things, like timidity, which quietly disintegrate the full field of life's possibilities.

In contrast, within the luminous spectrum of awareness, the most incandescent angel is the one who ignites joy. When a general state of good cheer prevails, man creates and radiates immaculate, benevolent revolutions. He reshapes his own existence, transforms his surroundings, and—most importantly—imprints a principled influence upon the world. The mind expands outward what contracts it within. When positive or negative thoughts are gathered, so too do actions unfold accordingly. Only those with a benevolent mindset can ease the atmosphere with a contagious enthusiasm.

If life appears to be an impossible mission, then falsehood is the covert agent, and the search for truth is what divulges it. Man is the being who negotiates his own lies, and at the same time, unconsciously, he bears wrath toward destiny for it refuses to sell him the truth. The imprudence of being dishonest with oneself, the betrayal of integrity, becomes the highest price one pays. Numbed by the fatigue of living alongside deception, he pleads life for something it cannot offer: mercy. Terrified by the prospect of waking without clemency, he prolongs his journey through the vicious cycle of dishonesty and cultivates an obsession with escaping reality; through means that ultimately corrupt his very being. All his problems are born in falsehood, because truth is like the atom, present in all things, the singular foundation upon which every element of the surrounding world is built. Lies, by contrast, are like dust, they settle, stain, and spoil. If we assume, even hypothetically, the notion claimed by some religions, that God created man from the dust of the earth, then perhaps we understand why falsehood defiles human existence: he has not been purified since creation.

Lying, in the end, becomes a passive resistance against destiny itself, a habitual indifference that leads one to a place where no calling offers solace. Only exactitude can displace the inessential dislocations from the steadfastness of fate, in service of exhaustion. What is false or true ceases to be a matter of inconsistency. And, one may ask, why does reality speak of sincerity, while illusion lends its ear to duplicity? Perhaps because life, as a condition of conception, favors authenticity: creation requires the real, only imitation relies on the false.

What is life? This question interweaves with every conscious soul. Many ask it, few reflect upon it, and almost no one echoes it. From childhood onward, with the first fierce pulses of personality, each of us stirs a vibration of individuality, instinctively compelled to understand what life means, and more so, what purpose it serves. In youth, we plunge into a ravenous hunger for knowledge, and external curiosity unsettles our peace. The interaction with the outside world becomes a source of pleasure, so long as the unknown remains untouched.

Childhood is a sequence of events lived without the anchor of experience, which is why memory remains laden with puerile recollections even into the twilight of old age. These are the moments when everything feels beautiful and free of care. Infant curiosity touches a kind of peak, a pinnacle of energetic intensity rarely matched later in life. No child ever reaches a saturation point when it comes to learning and discovery. For the young, learning is a preoccupation; for the old it becomes a propound.

The ability to gather and absorb knowledge about our world forms the very foundation upon which the future is built. The distinction between a flourishing society and one in decline lies not so much in the stable achievements of its adults, but in the exhaustive depth of education offered to its children. The adult's most profound societal impact resides in the relationship they nurture with their offspring. The child seeks to unlock the gate of knowledge, and the most immediate key is the parent.

Curiosity consumes oxygen at a high rate, and parents may often feel breathless, suffocated by an endless stream of questions of varying difficulty. The patience of a parent is the virtue of a child. Yet it must be said: a mother or father cannot answer every question, nor fully respond to every inquiry; only in some cases. The sheer variety of questions creates inevitable gaps in a child's understanding, for not all answers can match the depth of the questions posed. To a simple query such as "Why do birds fly?" the answer is straightforward and easily grasped by a young mind. But to questions like "Why are people cruel?" or "What is God?", the answers tend to deepen both confusion and curiosity.

Some are inclined toward the mystical, others toward the rational, and this duality grants the spectrum of knowledge an overwhelming and infinite ambiguity. Unreal answers, those unfounded in matter, especially those that cannot be seen, tasted, heard, touched, or smelled, subjects that elude the five senses, are the most fertile soil in which the enigma of existence deepens. A certain word echoes constantly, used by all, yet charged with more intrigue than any other: "life."

In the absence of clarity, driven by an obsession to purify human purpose, the quest to understand the essence and meaning of life becomes one's most faithful companion in moments of profound solitude. When the satisfaction of knowledge cannot be attained through conversation, there remains only the possibility of discovering it in solitude. Solitude becomes the ideal training ground for exceptional preparation, it is the only place where the rival is a partner, and hardship, a hidden advantage. In these social vacuums, thoughts begin to circulate in loops. Every question breeds another; every answer opens new dilemmas. The risk of losing direction and generating layers of confusion is high—and often realized. When a dilemma begins to stray from expectation, leading not to resolution but to a deeper descent into mystery, all that remains is to refine the method of seeking.

Thus, the approach must begin with what is concretely known about existence. It has a point of origin and a point of cessation. The interval between them, biologically defined, is called "life." With what distinguishes the human being in these two states? At birth, he knows nothing; at death, he understands little. These two certainties suggest at least a fragment of life's meaning, or perhaps its entire essence: to know, to learn, to experience—a beginning, and a direction.

Consequently, the consolidation of any orientation, intellectual, spiritual, or practical, shapes the subconscious, and the mind begins to remold itself, often without the individual's awareness. Over time, as a person evolves intellectually, familiar pleasures lose their spark; what once captivated now bores, and the fear of trying something new transforms into an attraction. Sooner or later, each of us comes to recognize that "experience" is no longer just a word that describes lessons earned through living, it becomes a pursuit in itself.

Experiences may be divided into two kinds: those extended within a singular domain, and those scattered across many. A concentrated experience leads one to excellence in a specific field but narrows the horizon, often at the expense of other depths. A diversified experience, on the other hand, broadens the world and its limits, but trades excellence for breadth. Experience spends unfulfillment to purchase vocation. It is a prolonged inclination toward emancipation and fruition.

It is difficult to say, precisely, universally, how many or why some people choose one path of experience over another. What is certain is that life builds itself through daily encounters. Some become consumed by a fascination with a sub-field, a branch emerging from the trunk of a larger pursuit, itself rooted in a greater domain: the vast tree of creation. The sap of obsession drives toward excellence in that branch.

There exists a kind of positive discrimination in society, especially toward those who reach the pinnacle of a given discipline. Talent is often praised, but the map that led to success remains largely concealed in the collective psyche. The path to excellence is owed, more often than not, to the labor and time invested in a craft, far more than to innate talent. There is only one credible forgery of glory: the exaggeration of talent.

There circulates, in society, a prevailing notion: that a modest number of practiced hours is enough to place an individual among a select elite; better than most, distinguished by ease. Yet this is a fallacy: a faint illusion, distant from the realm of true dedication. To truly rise to the top, certain individuals break through the very boundaries of limitation.

They enchant performance not through a calculable amount of effort, but through such an abundance of practice that counting ceases to matter. One who is sufficiently ambitious, who does not flirt with the idea of surrender, neither easily nor spontaneously, can excel in any pursuit.

In the flow of societal belief, there persist certain partial truths, unchallenged, yet incomplete, which steer life toward the fragmented fulfillment of what might otherwise be a complete, infinite realization. Many hold as gospel that motivation, discipline, devotion, perseverance, passion, focus, repetition, consistency, and intelligence are the essential virtues required to lead a grand, limitless life. And indeed, these are formidable qualities, stripped of superficiality. Anyone who dares to internalize them will go far.

But far does not mean near to the border of the infinite, nor does it mean brushing against perfection. It simply means reaching a place where the delight of achievement encounters a limit. Every constructive attitude is a fragment of truth, a brick in the edifice of purpose. In the architecture of a human life, the one absolute truth that shatters the wall of limitation is obsession.

Whenever a miraculous accomplishment appears, something extraordinary, or forged against the sheer impossibility of success, obsession is the total truth that justifies the inexplicable. Certainly, the more arduous virtues are part of the equation, but what fuses them, amplifies them, and stretches them into boundlessness is obsession. The most common madness is believing one can become the best without the mania of obsession.

Why is this worth highlighting? Because many live with aspirations of greatness and believe that a life governed by order and diligent effort is enough. And so, some endure the cruelest form of disillusionment, punished by their own dedication. They work tirelessly toward a goal, only to find themselves incapable of reaching that euphoric summit: of being the best, the first. The objectionable result is a peculiar and desolate bitterness.

Those gripped by obsession, who sleep and wake to the rhythm of a singular pursuit, whose very breath alternates with reflections on their fixation, are invincible. They operate on a plane beyond that of those who advance through structured order alone. Consider, for instance, how disciplined a person must be in a field such as chess to defeat another whose mind is entirely consumed, possessed, by the game. The answer lies as far as the finalization of the impossible. And yet, there is a danger: for those who have reached a certain level through effort alone, there can arise, suddenly and unexpectedly, a despair, a collapse that comes only when they realize they cannot surpass the obsessed. There is no suffering more profound than the failure to attain one's deepest longing, especially when much effort has already been spent. But the solution, though subtle, is not vague, it emerges from a vision of balance. One must not place expectations too far beyond one's standard of demand. Expectation is a premature overreach; exigency is the steady path of progress.

Yet there are those who simply cannot fuse with the idea of being fixated on a single pursuit. This inability reveals itself not only to others but, more critically, to the self. Parents may introduce their children to the specific tools of a craft, stimulate their interest, and provide the necessary means to practice and learn, but repetition does not resonate with everyone. For some, chemistry with obsession is like that between oil and water. Interest burns brightly at first, in the freshness of the beginning, but as time passes, the attraction fades, then boredom becomes unbearable and abrupt abandonment is inevitable.

These individuals belong to the second category: those who choose to experiment broadly, fully aware that they cannot be as combative or competitive as those who pour everything into the satirization of time, the art of repeatedly confronting a single domain to reveal its immanent essence. Every subtraction from ambition is an addition to resignation. Resignation is the ominous foresight of the inconsistent soul.

Yet, in certain rare cases, logic justifies withdrawal, for it may spare a person the absurdity of competing where they do not belong. In the spirit of competition, a person who falls asleep and awakens with a purpose in mind, a life tethered to a singular pursuit, will strip an amateur of humility only by deliberate intent. Perseverance, paired with failure and frustration, may gift a brave loser nothing but exasperation. Still, it is undeniable: the legitimacy of a winner stirs from the vanquished's unfulfilled desire to triumph. There is no grandeur in triumphing over someone who never gave everything for the win.

More to the point, the real loser is not the one who is defeated, but the one who ceases to evolve. More defeated than the defeated is the victor who has not improved. Therefore, the essence of failure lies not in defeat but in stagnation. Whenever something is gained, even in the aftermath of collapse, it is a form of success. Man can only be truly defeated by constancy and by regression.

Being first is not more important than being in the right race, the race with oneself. Put more clearly: no one competes with another human being. The true contest unfolds in the loneliness of one's own struggle against anonymity. It is a path of separation, of disassociation from the self that finds temporary comfort in stagnation. To wrestle with oneself is to dismantle life's inherent deviation, and this is vital if one is to escape the vices of existence.

Deviation from an authentic life, one that is untainted, grounded in truth, and clarified in vision, is punished by an inability to perceive even life's most obvious aspects. Perspective is not measured by what the eyes can see, but by the depths of thought. For a person admires outwardly only that which resonates inwardly. A darkened mind esteems a shadowed reality. An illuminated mind, in contrast, detests the seductive trap of illusion. Naturally, one's fit in existence depends upon a reflex of acceptance, reconciliation, or adaptation, how the mind aligns with the external world. No one can bear life while renouncing their own inner experience. No one who is not legitimizes the madness. And if it is not madness, then it is folly. A discord between one's mentality and lived experience forms the seedbed of despair, a despair that can only be deceived by the distortion of reality. And when one becomes lucid enough to recognize the incongruence, madness is often the only destination left. If inwardly one esteems luxury, yet outwardly embraces poverty, then one inevitably slanders their own existence, whether through sorrow, born of a life longed for yet unattainable, or through the silent foolishness that allows one to ignore the truth.

The absurdity of harboring pride while rejecting one's own life trajectory grants the lost individual a direction—one paved in disappointment. From this cynical disenchantment arises every struggle related to the mental acceptance of insufficiency. Truthfully, a darkened mind does not burden the spirit; it seals it, ushering life into the cramped comfort of dead ends.

There are those who ask whether anything in this universe carries meaning, whether their existence is merely an accidental absurdity. In reality, the entire challenge is to accept life as it is, both the blessings and the burdens. With every refusal to do so, one inches closer to nonexistence. Lacking the courage to face the truth, such individuals fracture their relationship with themselves. Life does not compel us to lie, it simply distorts our understanding. And with a distorted judgment, perception becomes chronic.

A delusional framework emerges either from falsehood or the over-amplification of a minor truth. A person with the slightest physical imperfection, a small deviation in the nose, may perceive it as grotesque. The resulting psychological impact distorts their vision of themselves and brings about deep emotional suffering. Though others see nothing wrong, the individual's self-awareness collapses, and self-esteem erodes. This condition is called body dysmorphia.

If there exists an illness that transforms the normal into ugliness in the physical realm, could there not also be one that distorts the intangible, our very experience of life? Why shouldn't a person also suffer from a *life dysmorphia*—a perception of life as more repugnant or painful than it truly is?

All people suffer from some form of dysmorphia. No one lives with a perfectly symmetrical vision of reality. A simple realization, an organic deviation from perfectionism, should normalize the presence of flaws to the extent that absolutist thinking becomes improper. Those who refuse to accept life with its defects admit, in essence, their discomfort with belonging to the seductive reality of existence. Once seduced, the human spirit, detached from the organic flow of imperfection, reinterprets reality as catastrophe.

It is a disastrous belief to entreat imperfection as deficiency rather than normality; such thinking signals a sterile relationship with lucidity. Some live in awareness of their flaws, others fail to comprehend them, and still others multiply them in their minds. In neither perfection nor deformity is there freedom, for in the former, there is no room for error, and in the latter, no escape from it. One's independence is thus measured by neutrality in the face of polarizing experiences.

Life demands equidistance, a balanced determination that comforts rather than condemns. People often say "no one is perfect," yet few recognize that all suffer from dysmorphias. Perfection is unattainable, but dysmorphia can be distanced through adaptation. There is no one who does not perceive some bodily flaw, no one fully content with their form, and nearly everyone expands their perception of ugliness beyond its reality—gaining modesty but losing confidence in the process. And body dysmorphia is only the beginning, life dysmorphia is just as normative, as is that of love. No one would long for a more perfect partner if they did not deem the one they have more flawed than they can grant. Dysmorphic thinking, by its disproportion and distortion, feeds subjectivity, a kind of awakening from the real. And for this reason, *life dysmorphia* drains authenticity from consciousness, eclipsing the present moment without invoking finality. Everyone touched by the harsh light of truth, by the direct contact with objectivity, retreats into the comfort of subjectivity, a domain that stirs them inwardly, until they reshape the entire world in their own image. It is a shift in perception, a full immersion into the self, where the world floats in one's private dream and the mind spills into the illusion of clarity beneath the veil of hope.

The human being, as a wandering creature, might best be described this way: not as one who transforms himself to meet the demands of reality, but as one who waits, often futilely, for reality to bend to his desires. If he does not discern what life asks of him, and instead bombards it with endless, undefined demands, then all his longing becomes a philosophical endeavor to embrace the sensation of the unreal. There is no one who has not, at least once, pursued something inherently unachievable, thus, no one has been spared the disorientation that follows a sincere surrender.

All forms of disorientation are but symbols of inner deviation, and as such, every individual structure of personhood has experienced some degree of deformation. And yet, beyond this fact—beyond the diffuse and extrasensory plane—there remains that gaze, which once glimpsed beauty within the unreal. That gaze is universal, intense and alluring, for it feeds the personal illusion of possible transformation.

The core of human difficulty is not the height of one's expectations, but the scarcity of one's actions. Deeds are the unknowns that never resolve the equation of hope. So long as man fails to understand his proportional weight in existence, he will dwell in the convoluted entanglement of the unachievable. All people place more faith in hope than they do in action; this alone explains the ubiquity of life dysmorphia. As hope and expectation swell while action and accomplishment shrink, the middle ground becomes the breeding ground for dissatisfaction, distorting the world into something uglier than it is.

There is only one way to sever friendship with life: by seeking revenge upon it. And there is but one method to do so: by lying to oneself.

Today, humanity lives in the most favorable era in recorded history—undeniably, without dispute. And this very truth overwhelms many. Prolonged peace, social and economic progress, advancements in medicine and technology, every dimension of civilized life has undergone profound transformation. One could even claim, with some justification, that the objective harshness of reality has diminished. Which implies an entire complex of new emotional dispositions.

As society evolves, each person's emotional compass is tested, and whether they wish it or not, they are forced to adapt to new standards of coexistence. To grasp the full meaning of this shift, one must draw a parallel through time: what life once was, and what it has become. This comparison gives rise to a sobering realization: those born closest to the present enjoy an unearned advantage. Unearned, for they contributed nothing to create it; they simply emerged at a fortunate moment in history. Time itself imposes well-being upon them, and they grow bitter in response.

A simple person today lives better than a nobleman did a century ago. Billions have lived before us, yet those alive now make up a small fraction of all humanity, and they are the most fortunate. From the dawn of humankind, how many had the luxury of a chosen vacation? A climate-controlled home? The certainty that food would not spoil? Easy access to clothing for all seasons, or tools to simplify daily life? How many worked under humane conditions?

Who, before now, carried in their pocket a device to hear the voice of loved ones anytime, anywhere? Who traveled so easily? Who woke in the morning knowing what the weather would be at night? Who had access to medical services at their fingertips? The list is endless. But what matters most emerges clearly from this historical contrast: human health has reached unprecedented security. In the past, a simple fracture might mean lifelong disability. Worse still is the cruel truth that millions once suffered the most devastating grief, losing a child, because infant mortality was common before the rise of modern medicine. How many women and children once waited, uncertain whether their husbands or fathers would return from war? How many had access to information as readily as we do today, where even the deepest problems can be unearthed in seconds? And so the questions continue. What remains essential is drawn not from speculation, but from the contrast between then and now.

Upon a thorough dissection of history, it becomes impossible to deny that the present shelters humanity in the most favorable of times. And what we know of the past is but a summary, an abridged version of a far more brutal, unfiltered story. The man who falls from the grace of the present does not bow to the disfavor of the past. Why, then, is he tormented by privilege? Why does he call life ugly, when it has never been better than it is now? If he lives through the most beautiful of ages yet exaggerates life's unpleasantness, can we not conclude, at least in theory, that he suffers from a kind of *life dysmorphia*?

Life feels heavy when you seek significance. It becomes light when you find irrelevance. It appears ugly when you demand greatness. It turns beautiful when clarity arrives. It grows complex when you act with lucidity. It simplifies when you accept the absurdity of existence. Everything, in the end, is a pretext—an excuse to justify one's happiness or despair.

Nothing external can redeem man from the ridiculous impulse to legitimize his failure to understand a world overwhelmed by its own motion. Only when he confronts the boundaries of life, when he finally understands that strength is the consensual release from living in disharmony with all possible states, will he abandon the embarrassing habit of assigning adjectives to life. To label life is to attempt to calculate the ratio of the irrational, a futile exercise. Existence must be balanced within the philosophy of the self; to cling to only one part of perception is to remain stranded. Without philosophy, reality becomes distorted through the illusion of destiny. How compact fate appears when one contemplates the infinite scale of the universe, and yet life reduces itself to the ability of any one person to reshape reality within a spaceless dimension, one that expands as wildly as the human mind itself. To be a philosopher is to be wise without honoring the Universe's confidentiality.

There are only three kinds of people: those who believe the world revolves around them; those who feel lost in space; and those who believe in a vacuum of meaning, floating aimlessly in chance. Perhaps one of the greatest injustices of the Universe is the misalignment of people in history. Some endured horrors to build a paradise they would never live to see, while others stumbled into that paradise having done nothing for its creation. Divinity holds in reserve only one supreme act of justice: to reverse time. That those who lived through darkness might also live through light, and those born into light might come to know the dark. Humanity shows no gratitude for the tragedy of advantage. But perhaps, with a proper reward, people would cease to take revenge on happiness, and instead, forgive it from within their pain.

Indeed, there are those with grave reasons to lament life, those who endure conscious suffering. But for many, tears arise merely as condensation from the fog of the mind. True suffering is that which causes one to forget oneself entirely. A terrible sensation, felt like a phantom within, erupting into the void of one's being—crushing consciousness beneath the weight of a dreadful question: *"Why is the world so cruel, so filled with suffering and injustice?"*

When suffering revolves solely around one's own lack, it becomes a mental torment, an illusion that expands indefinitely while contracting into the ego. This kind of unhappiness, brewed in the pursuit of personal needs, is fundamentally self-centered. Individual pain can be managed; collective suffering can only be accepted. That is why personal misfortunes can be endured, because one remains part of the equation and holds some power to balance the outcome. But the same cannot be said for tragedies that exclude the self: the illness of a child, natural catastrophes, war, social horrors, or disasters that engulf entire communities—these are the genuine sorrows that dissolve the ego. Even an incurable illness becomes most painful not in isolation, but in the thought of those who love you.

On the other hand, when someone accuses life of withholding happiness because of a personal setback, the feeling often lacks true depth, it is more often a fabrication spun in the auditorium of the mind. It frequently links to comforting falsehoods: luck, chance, misfortune, destiny. If someone claims to be unhappy because fate has been unkind, what choices remain? To linger in melancholy, or to challenge adversity; because with ambition and perseverance, even fate can be softened.

Thus, what man knows yet does not understand is this: suffering must be carried through to its end. Until he ceases to measure its length with dramatic precision, and shortens his vanity about what happiness should be. If one desires happiness at all costs, then one must pay the price of suffering's revenge. Such a tribute makes one a captive to the cost imposed by privilege itself.

People demand favor, as though the simple fact of being alive were not already a magnificent gift. And not just any favor, but one substantial enough to impress them. Perhaps they would better endure a life full of misfortune if their thoughts were not so obsessed with deciphering meaning. Not all people grasp meaning, and thus, not all are truly unhappy. Ultimately, all that the mind fuses into a tangle of significance contributes to the mentality that constantly re-evaluates the validity of illusion. The true tragedy of life is that recognition precedes knowledge. People identify a goal before they even explore it, and thus, what they imagine in advance becomes nothing more than a bitter projection. How else does the man comes to yearn for surrender even before the summon is made?

Still, one cannot help but admire the tenacity with which some overinflate thought in the simple act of living. It is an invincible form of obstinacy and individuation; to believe the world begins and ends with the self. And perhaps, the one who stirs the wind of self-love does not exaggerate the world, but himself.

What is a superman? Truly, who can know? And what is more terrifying: to accept reality as it is, or to admire illusion for all that it is not? Reality is what is—a kind of inferno—for the unimportant man and the unloved woman. But reality is also what is not—something that can be interpreted—for one kind of person: the philosopher. The definition of philosophy emerges when a great affirmation erupts from an unassuming allegation.

The veil of life is the individual destiny, forever cloaked in mystery. The last mortal who inwardly believes he has seen and understood everything is, in truth, at war with the regret that life will not allow him to perpetuate his own existence. In the end, no one can journey to life's conclusion armed only with stubbornness, for it is always lost along the way, and profoundly so. Sooner or later, everyone arrives at that impasse where time must be lived in detail, and over them, acceptance gently descends. Only a soul afflicted by repulsion can rehabilitate the epilogue of an ending it never consented to. It becomes necessary to conform to solace if one hopes to avoid conversion into the ontological dimension of melancholy.

In life, the question is never truly about reconciliation, or even the avoidance of conflict, but rather about adopting an attitude of understanding toward the unknown. It's implied that any relationship with something unknowable demands an investment of time, a notion that falls into correspondence with reason, even though reason finds perfection fantastical. The pursuit of perfection, in the presence of the axiom *"No one is perfect,"* becomes an act of rebellion within the contract of life. But rebellion is short-lived. Hunted by exhaustion, man must eventually yield to a regret: that he is destined to evolve within imperfection. It would be against the very fabric of nature, unintelligible, to aim for a faultless existence. And should he try, he succeeds only in intensifying the illusion. This is why the fascination with what is ugly makes him shine. Leave the ugly untouched, and it dissipates. A painful event clings only through absorption. For suffering, neglect is a secretion of venom, while attention is a dose of vitamins.

Why is it that, for some, everything, absolutely everything, is subjected to reason? The Latins had a phrase: *Nihil sine Deo*—"Nothing without God." The unfortunate have their own motto: *"Nothing without prejudice."* In this way, judgment becomes fundamental to the perception of beauty and ugliness. Animals cannot conceive of defects or perfection. Only man, in his turmoil, is capable of stirring the waters further. But why does he do so? Why is he tormented by a minor flaw in the nose and yet unmoved by the perfection of the eyes? Why does he taste the flavor of life with bitterness?

They are all *"whys"*, but none are *"hows."* And *how* else can a *why* be understood if not through a *how*? One cannot arrive at *"Why did he come to suffer from life dysmorphia?"* without first unraveling *"How did he begin down that path?"* And to truly understand why he savors the ugly and the beautiful is swallowed, one must examine life through its flavors. Seven chosen essences: time, freedom, happiness, love, success, wealth, and faith.

2

Time

The universe: the place furthest from transience, and closest to eternity. With its infinite ego, it is an astral being, trilateral in nature, composed of space, matter, and time. Within it, energy flows as cosmic blood, sustaining its endlessness, its unconditioned essence, its limitlessness, and its ceaseless motion. Existence itself depends on the interrelationship of these three—none fulfilling its role without the others. This is a contract, without which nothing would hold meaning.

Hypothetically, the universe unfolds within a triangle, whose vertices are space, time, and matter. To each of these dimensions, one might, through philosophical excess, assign a sub-dimension: *where*, *when*, and *what*. Time and matter, without space, would be lost. Time and space, without matter, would be void. Matter and space, without time, would be ended. From each vertex of the triangle, energy draws a line inward, and where those lines meet lies the singular point of reality, the moment of existence, the essence of everything: the eye that beholds the infinite. Yet beyond the physical framework, within this point of convergence, arises the greatest philosophical dimension of all: *"why?"*

This surplus of harmony transcends the idea that life is meaningless. But there remains one thing the laws of the universe do not reveal: purpose. No human can understand their purpose through the theoretical study of nature alone. *"Why does life exist?"*—this remains the eternal meditation of philosophers and mystics. And from the moment purpose reveals itself, whether through insight or revelation, man realizes that everything is a concept veiled in emptiness. The privilege of living, indissoluble, can be reduced to one phrase: to become insusceptible to limitation.

In time, all come to understand that life is but a slice of time carved into the continuum, and in the end, the acceptance of this truth quiets the desperate need to find meaning. Yet let us not dismiss despair—it, too, has its place. For unless you've never laid a hand on despair, you will never truly feel what life means.

Every creature develops, to varying degrees, the ability to govern space (location) and matter (living or nonliving things). But in the face of time, all surrender, even willingly, any attempt of controlled rebellion. Because existence is ultimately confined to the consumption of a period, every moment becomes charged with meaning, and no instant can be relegated to nullity.

Resignation, whether by choice or necessity, appears when one reaches a state of living that no longer feels the urgency of being pressed by time. Thus, purpose is not a natural phenomenon; it is not written into the equations of the Universe. It emerges within the consciousness of living beings as an invitation into existence, arriving only when time gazes, patient and quiet, upon those burning with the need to survive; seeking a reason to live. Animals are not conscious of time's presence, yet they act in instinctual harmony with nature to persist. Man, on the other hand, is lifted by reason above the speechless beasts. He is lucid to the passing of seconds, aware that all things end, and in that awareness, he complicates what is otherwise a simple impulse, to survive, by transforming it into the urge to *create meaning*. The individual who forsakes creation and disregards the passing moments becomes nothing more than an unfulfilled animal, condemned to endure the prison of existence, from which only death may offer exculpation.

Beneath the sword of time, man abdicates his yearning to crown himself a god. The final cravings for power are severed by the closeness of his destiny, to reign not over the living, but in the realm of the inanimate. Without an end, life would lose its essence. It would become a brutal rivalry with the Divine, a punishment of having to endure eternity—and, at the same time, would poison every opportunity to wander freely through the paradise of fulfillment. The charm of life lies in its temporality. The joy of living with fervor begins in the stubborn defiance of the inevitable end. Love, happiness, freedom, success—these are lived with immeasurable intensity. Yet, these are but a paradox: to experience within infinity something that ultimately has an end. Consider love, for instance: if it never ended, it would become a sentence of eternal fatigue; because every kiss is a release from the prison of fleeting time.

Had man been granted dominion over time, he would have

forsaken his humanity and all that drifts with it—usurping the place of the Supreme Being. In the absence of immortality, he remains a humble traveler through the world, a creator with limited, relative, and temporary powers, a sentimental fugitive fleeing the claws of reality, and in the end, a daily witness to his own approaching disappearance.

No one holds the privilege of escaping the ticking of the clock; at best, one can ignore it. People may detach from many things, but they cannot nullify time's unrelenting passion for annihilating existence. Indeed, humanity as a whole follows but one thread: the course of time. Gods may be denied, people renounced, identities shed, but the flow of history clings to all.

In the absence of "*chronocide*," or an exit through time's gates, man has but one noble way to respond to this temporal struggle: to leave his imprint on the scroll of chronology. If we are all fated to vanish into a pure despair, perhaps the most sublime path to eternalizing a life in resonance with time is to leave a trace—otherwise, history finds itself too easily relieved of the burden of praising humanity.

History lulls regret; the future awakens hope. In the idealism of the universe, time is always *now*. Past and future are gravitational constructs born of the human need to measure the weight of chronology. One is veiled in memory, the other in imagination. On this axis arranged by the order of temporal succession, man stands in the present, and he bears no human aspect, for he walks facing the future while his gaze remains fixed on the past.

As a remedy against living in the moment, he instinctively leans one way or another, forward or backward, thus losing contact with the present, the only true consumable expression of time. Both the leaning toward the future and the clinging to the past are, in equal means, ways of losing time. Time can only be redeemed by splitting each moment open. "*I'll do it tomorrow*" is the twin brother of "*I didn't do it yesterday.*" The mother of all creation is *"I do it now."*

Interest in memory or imagination may bring one closer to revelation, but it cannot carve history without immediate action. Thus, without deed, *what was* remains nostalgia, and *what could have been* becomes a lost hope.

Passivity is physiological. Life often manifests as a quiet curiosity, an urge to wait. Those who lose patience are the ones who begin to uncover the secrets of time. In a world governed by the logic of chaos, where nothing can be precisely anticipated, where the smallest detail can shift the entire course of what is to come, where each second can reshape decades—what could be more reckless than *waiting*?

Nature does not reward inaction; it punishes it. Animals, unaware of time's existence, are spared the opportunity to waste it. A lion does not sit idle, waiting for its prey to arrive at its mouth, it moves when necessity demands. But in the realm of reason, man accumulates days with no result, lives in a state of active indifference, delays immediate action, and waits for time itself to deliver resolution, as though life were bound by contract and destiny were obliged to provide favorable returns.

Meanwhile, human life expectancy hovers around 80 years, a span some view as generous, others as brief. Measured in years, time appears expansive, abundant. But when translated into days, perception sharpens. Eighty years equals roughly 29,000 days. That number is not large. And once the already-lived days are subtracted, what remains is a shrinking sum, cosmically insignificant, and yet, with each passing day, all the more precious.

Each day is a resource without replacement. A lost day is a missed opportunity—a fleeting insufficiency of occasion. Without a present, daily heroism, the past will be persecuted, and the future, squandered.

The future is merely a versatile past. Afflicted by regret, people would trade anything for divine intervention, something to rewrite history, to nullify their mistakes, to be granted mercy before the harsh truth: once something is done, it cannot be undone. Time consumed is irreversible. It must be accepted. And yet, there remains a curious consolation, man can alter an untouched past: the one flattered under the name *future*. In the collective mind, tomorrow belongs to the future. But in not much time at all, tomorrow will change its conceptual shape and be reclassified as the past, specifically, the day before yesterday.

Man is not eager to swim through time; he merely allows time to flow through him. Every second, minute, day, month, or year manifests like a symptom of creation's illness, its inherent relativism. Yet within every person lies the power to dilate or contract the unfolding of events, to wrestle with the uncertainty of succession. Without human intervention, history would be nothing more than trivial protocol in the face of chaos.

Certainly, no being can wholly purify disorder, but one can, to a degree, dispel uncertainty, regret, despair, or unfasten the knots that appear as links in the chain of causality. The anticipation of the future is only possible through the fragmentation of chaotic sequences. A future desired becomes a past delivered.

All forms of remorse weigh heavily on existence, and they are born from the vast field of inaction. Regrets resemble wrinkles: they deepen and multiply with age. This is perhaps why the most humming advantage of childhood is immunity to remorse. Maturity becomes symptomatic, marked by the growing virulence of self-reproach.

A person at the age of 30, in theory, may have 50 years left to live. These 50 years offer a supreme opportunity: the chance to mold each act of life according to personal aspiration. Thus, one who reaches the age of 80 may escape the torment of wasted time, and carry a memory unburdened by deep regrets. In this way, the future becomes a past worth remembering, made notable through the effect of the present.

As a visual paradox, man sees the most in *nothing*. He who wastes the most time claims he has no time for anything. He who is destitute insists he needs nothing. He who loves no one declares he requires nothing. He who has seen little says nothing can impress him. And so the examples multiply. In the absence of everything, nothingness fills the void. Through this mourning of lack, all become enslaved by a failure born of limitation. They elevate it. They magnify it. An illusion of significance, when in truth, reality speaks the opposite. Admiration for emptiness only burdens the soul with unused possibilities.

Thus, when a person does *nothing*, time weighs most heavily upon them. In contrast, when one is active, time becomes light—forgotten. The relative perception of time is directly tied to action: without deed, the ticking becomes oppressive; with activity, the passing hours soften. The formula for calculating duration becomes meaningless unless it begins from an equation in which the result is accomplishment. What value is there in counting the hours of a day in which nothing was done? It is a question hurled into irrelevance. Only he who bites into the prepared dish of time may be poisoned by its value. All that belongs to chronology cries out for an accounting in hours of creation. Nothingness silences history, smallness sniffs at it, and the wholeness feels it.

Time reveals itself as a cruel phenomenon to the one most condemned to endure a deprivation of freedom. No, not the prisoner, but the insomniac. The principal role of sleep is not rest, but disconnection from reality. All people show weakness in facing prolonged lucidity, and sleep is what keeps us from sliding into madness. That break in consciousness, a severing from the burdens of the world, where worry, chaos, and pain cease to be processed, is the noblest form of liberation.

Sleep is the most transparent way of honoring time, a mechanism for keeping reason from turning opaque. In its absence, the first thing that unravels is the peace of the present moment; every second spent in bed becomes a battleground. Insomnia is the clash of thoughts. From that battle, one may emerge victorious or defeated, thus, not all sleeplessness is wasted time. Yet it remains the most harrowing way to spend it, when one can. For many, sleeplessness has unlocked moments of creation; for others, it opened the door to suffering. It's well known that numerous artists, inventors, writers, and scientists found their ideas completed in moments of wakeful unrest, just as many others lost theirs the same way. Moment and thought share a common trait: their velocity from presence to disappearance.

Time also stirs ethical conflict between historical periods. It enlists all people into the army of death and arms collective consciousness with the weapon of relativism. Physical disappearance from this world is inevitable, no one can play truant forever. Yet a human presence can persist beyond the body through the greatness of thought. Mentality detaches one being from another and attaches a life to an era. Every person belongs to a time, both in body and in mind. In death, one may still speak—*but only if there is a story to tell.* Otherwise, one falls eternally silent.

The most crucial social artifact born of thought is morality. It is the balance by which good and evil are weighed in the moment, and it alone holds the power to cleanse society of many of its toxins. Unfortunately, this balance can be disrupted when its center of gravity is eroded by time. Morality becomes, in some cases, a superficial subjectivity when inserted between historical contexts. One cannot judge the past by the morality of the present, or dismiss the idea that what is right today may be wrong tomorrow. Social standards are like water: they take the shape of the vessel that contains them—the collective. And so, people often show dishonesty in their dissection of history. They place it on trial, hurling modern judgments at it, forgetting that to understand is greater than to condemn. Most dissociate from the mistakes of the past, especially political ones, but few attempt to understand why people believed they were on the right path at the time. Even fewer attempt a genuine exercise in empathy: to place themselves inside that era, with its education, its customs, its limitations, and ask: Would I have thought differently? Would I have stood against it? Or stood with it?

Each day, an intellectual routine asserts itself: people

emerge, ideas arise, arguments are made, philosophies shift. And so collective perception evolves, and thought cannot remain inert under time's momentum. Thus, morality changes gradually as one era transitions into another. And for that reason, people should be cautious when blaming history; instead, they should learn from it. In time, they too will be judged by generations to come. What is deemed moral today may one day be considered immoral; thoughts, actions, and even entire systems of society.

Chronology, as it unfolds, is shaped predominantly by malevolent significance. Human fascination with negation, with evil, has carved a history where the grim is boldly emphasized, and the beautiful fades into monotony. We know much about war, but little about peace. Killers bask in fame; founders vanish into obscurity. Destruction attracts attention; creation invites indifference. Time evaporates like a volatile liquid that reacts with reverence only to what is harmful. No wonder, time itself carries a fatal valence. It is, after all, history's greatest murderer. Hence humanity's deep obsession with it. Time has a throne reserved in Hell, implying that only Heaven may lay claim to eternity.

Sensitivity to misfortune is not a curse. It does not stem solely from the merciless dynamism of suffering. It arises from a deficiency in inner fortitude, a subtle exercise in human frailty. Consider this: two friends embark on a mountain journey. One is strong, the other weak. At a certain moment, they face an obstacle, a difficult situation. The strong one overcomes it with ease, gives it no weight, and continues his ascent. The weak one, however, struggles, freezes, succumbs to panic, and calls for help. At the journey's end, they will recount two vastly different experiences. The strong will speak of joy, of harmony with nature, of landscapes, pleasure, and discovered beauty. The weak will narrate a tale centered on torment, the pivotal moment being his own personal suffering, glossing over the good. History, then, is a story compelled to recount the tears of human weakness. In the theater of time, joy is a mere extra. Not even eternity can fortify human fragility, but it does offer the consolation of being tethered to the flow of events, a place where evolutionary senselessness finds its sanctuary.

The caprice of time manifests itself as a persistent harassment, desperate, aggressive, and reiterated through every lived experience. A fabrication, a social construct. It is what we call age. Spiritually, life is not measured in years but in the accumulation of experiences and feelings, stepping stones toward a state of closure, a reconciliation with the imbalance of 'enough,' a kind of self-negation of freshness. Life, in this regard, is the embodiment of consumption and a compound of creation. What can truly be said about the life of an 80-year-old? Not much, unless lived deeply. Age, then, becomes a flawed indicator, an informational handicap about any living being.

How did people relate to life before the invention of the calendar? Without comparison. Can two individuals, both aged fifty, be equated in experience? Hardly. It is both fascinating and humbling that humanity's brightest mathematicians and physicists have dared to tackle the infinitude of the universe, formulating it, theorizing it, even attempting to disprove its boundlessness. Yet they are often rendered mentally paralyzed by the idea that a human being can conduct an infinite number of calculations based on a single figure: their age. The mind refuses to rest. It cannot cease its relentless tallying of life's worth through this one persistent metric. If age were removed from consciousness, people might live freely, unburdened by the count of years. Years are the brake on the vibration of vitality.

It's not about the natural biological passage of time, because after all, even an aging lion hunts until its final day. But man, willingly, begins to stifle his own hopes, ambitions, and opportunities, all in deference to a single thing: his years.

Measuring a life is a process of infinite knowledge. It is deceptive, even tragic, to reduce it to a number. Only a fool values existence more than experience, elevating the weight of a year over the fullness of a moment. The instant fulfills, while the span debates. Life's essence does not demand an obsession with duration, but an attentiveness to the now. Only humans celebrate a sublime solar cycle while sighing between sunrise and sunset. The passing of a year is marked with festivity, while the passing of a day is washed away without ceremony. Thus, man remains the prisoner of a passive phenomenon, one that replaces temporary reality with permanent imagination, a thirst to consume time in the abstract rather than in presence. Everything is passionately scheduled into the future, as if distance dilutes duty, and the present is endured only as a placeholder for what is planned. Fundamentally, human life comes down to choosing whether to kill time or to fertilize it.

Goals that are always stretched out far ahead, are fostering a perilous comfort in delay. It's always "Next year I'll quit smoking," never "Today I stop." "Next year I'll marry, have a child, change careers." And so on. The failure lies not in planning, but in misunderstanding a brutal truth: passion is fleeting. One cannot affix desire onto the future when time itself is a remedy against enthusiasm—a kind of dragging the fervent into the rain. An emotional flame must be acted upon as close as possible to ignition, or it cools into apathy. And so the years pass, age accumulates, and plans remain embryonic. Without concrete results or a long-term horizon, man begins to obsessively repeat, "There isn't much time left." And from a certain age onward, each year digested is flavored with melancholy.

Experience is the disciple, time the academy, and the greatest masters are pain, suffering, danger, labor, and action. An exceptional, resilient, and complete human being can only be one who has intimately known adversity. In the absence of hardship, a person finds themselves wearing an incomplete character, especially in those crucial moments where skill has not been previously refined by contact. The weak suffer intensely from inexperience. They sweeten the act of living only with pleasure, comfort, or distraction. The strong, however, possess a broader palate: they savor every flavor, whether sweet, sour, bitter, spicy, or salty; without retching at life's diverse offerings.

Life is self-service, age a plate to be filled with experiences, and time changes the menu. Fulfillment comes from tasting every dish, every opportunity. To gain strength and wield power is a matter of proper nourishment. Weakness is not a mystery; it's the byproduct of avoidance and abstention. Time lays out a feast, yet man declines or evades it. Freshness cannot be preserved; everything spoils in the echo of ticking seconds. Eventually, too late, the man confesses his neglect and sniffs the scent of regret. Remorse spreads like a toxin of the mind, untouchable by antidotes, immune to even the healing passage of time. The only path to fulfillment lies in the privilege of using discomfort, or at least mimicking contentment. Experience elevates the strong; it governs the weak. Life's lessons are taught through suffering, and its teachers repeat the curriculum; until death rings the final bell.

Old age is the illness that finally cures one of something bothersome: too much time. Youth is an asymptomatic condition of time's malady. Paradoxically, a person reaching old age begins a new life, one in which the torment of planning dissolves, the seduction of wasted moments fades, experience overrules providence, and destiny gives real meaning to the word *rest*. Rest is fluid only for the young, but if saturated with excess time, it stagnates into a mire of laziness. Clearly, one cannot be both young and fully fulfilled in life, which renders the discovery of life a fleeting ecstasy. Insatiable longing and impulsive reaction are traits of the unformed, the immature.

The old and the young differ in hope and mirror each other in disillusionment. Both distort the weight of time: one overvalues it, the other underestimates it; one squanders it, the other clutches it with trembling hands. In youth, the direct link to failure is forged through the hope of a better future, a deception that improvises the present, where today is the victim and tomorrow the imagined hero. It's a self-imposed illusion, born of believing time is plentiful. In old age, the hope of enduring *today* becomes the bridge to *tomorrow,* and presence begins to resemble disappointment, not because of naive expectations of a long future, but due to the fading certainty that tomorrow will even arrive. Man lives puzzled by the significance of moments, holding a ticket to the theater of his own existence, where the grand performance is the life of one who lives in thought with time, but acts outside of it.

No one finds a complete face within, only outside. Everything that exists beyond the self defines the individual. But what is more difficult to change: a face molded by others or one sculpted by time itself? A person's character cannot remain untouched by external influences. Within every rational being lies a fragment of identity that was grafted onto them, unchosen. Moments, people, actions, events, consequences, each discord with inner constancy, leave their mark. And thus, as time passes, we all come to see: we are no longer who we once were. This is the revelation of becoming unique. Even the greatest recluse cannot speak from the height of a wholly self-fashioned identity.

We are defined by the past, built in the present, and altered by the future. Each passing day carves traces, physical and moral alike, and no one can claim they are wholly themselves without stepping beyond their own boundaries. Human interactions and fleeting moments are never truly random; every connection knots itself into the thread of one's life. Where one is born, their friends, religion, family, career, and conditions of existence—all of these become fountains that wear down the innocence we are born with. Maturity arises as a consequence of countless interweavings; it stands in direct contrast to the illusion that we can reject all external input. Time has blessed us with change, and yet man curses it. The future is premiering for who present the past as begin to be outdated.

The very notion of change unsettles human nature, evolution or regression disrupts what man mythologizes: a fixed identity. Yet the destiny of every person is marked by the constant oscillation of transformation over time. We may resist it, but we cannot amend it, only adapt, and that, only if it springs from a sincere inner will. So then, to shield oneself from an undesired, derivative identity, one must engage in the battle of transformation.

Time's volatility guarantees one thing: total uncertainty. It can be invested wisely, wastefully—or not at all. When the mind is turned toward growth, love, accomplishment, or meaning, each moment absorbs worth. But when bent toward distraction, indulgence, convenience, or vice, those same moments fill only with lightness; and in inaction, all turns hollow. Still, what might be the best investment of time? What should be the first priority? These are questions permitted only in the realm of imagination. No one can know the answer before they attempt, before they discover the inclination of their own nature. Not all are sentimental, pragmatic, moderate, or sociable, differences are guaranteed, which is making the discovery of a universal formula for life impossible. After all, what good would it do an elephant to learn how to hide?

But can one truly deny that the most vital and widespread hunger for life is, indisputably, the desire to dwell in love? How else might time be more divinely spent than as a slope down which one glides into the intoxicating sensation of affection? When love teaches, man tends to shirk life's lessons. No amount of knowledge can substitute for a deficiency in a relationship. And nothing is more profoundly inhuman than chewing through time in an endless solitude.

Loneliness does not burn unless it is seasoned with the absence of love. The effect of love upon the human being is that it softens regret in the grand equation of existence. Life without love equals a multitude of sorrows. The most grounded and unmistakable expression of being human occurs when one loves. Any orientation toward something else may reduce a person to less than human—or, at times, elevate them to more.

With this said, one might conclude, perhaps with deliberate bias, that the finest investment of time is in the pursuit and preservation of love. If a relationship has no duration, it must be begun. And if one is already unfolding, the time of love must be satisfying. If it is not, then both energy and time must be funneled toward a singular aim: to vitalize it.

The purest form of trivializing time, the act of injecting absurdity into duration, is neither in its neglect nor in its exploitation, but rather in the acceleration of events. Life is a fortunate accident, and speed is its prime accomplice. For many, time conforms to the metaphor of a road: it begins at point A, birth, and ends at point B, death. Yet this road is not measured in distance, but in duration. More than that, the illusion of a destination frees man from a slow unraveling into disorientation.

The beauty of life does not lie in the planning of the journey; it unfolds through the emergence of unexpected voyages. A meticulous arrangement of steps, seasons, and stops runs counter to the essence of living. Man cannot be stripped of the unpredictable nor bound to precision; he is destined to move alongside chaos. The singularity of time in the architecture of the universe arises from its contemplative relativity. The chronological path lacks a clear destination, but abounds in endless excursions. Being relative, this flow of time becomes the only road that cannot be shortened nor finished through speed, its core is deciphered through haste. In an ordinary journey, one reaches the end faster by moving quickly. But in time's orchestration, every arrival only leads to expansion; each end is the beginning of another.

Man's most formidable ability lies in his capacity to accelerate, for through speed, events unfold with heightened frequency. The faster he goes, the further he may reach in life, bringing to completion more endeavors. A steady pace will get one somewhere, and it outlasts inconsistency, but it can never outmatch velocity in action. A life crowned with many triumphs rises beneath the sword of swiftness.

3

Freedom

Freedom taunts man to a perpetual battle with existence. In the collective consciousness, it is an ideal, one whose importance is never questioned. Society's obsession with the overuse of the word *"freedom"* is understandable, for the deprivation of it runs contrary to human nature. Man was born to be free, yet paradoxically, and perhaps disturbingly, freedom overwhelms him. As the only creature aware of its existence, man lives burdened by it, and any detachment from it disturbs his inner equilibrium. The quarrel with freedom descends like a curtain of fog, separating the wanderer from life itself, submerging him in a haze of uncertainty.

The subconscious does not remain indifferent to this tension. It presses inward with a heavy, silent urgency for reconciliation, yet the path toward liberation is obstructed by the human condition itself—by weakness, by cowardice. To step out of bondage requires will.

Courage is the most vital steroid of freedom. To be free is

an exalted state, primarily of the mind. It is when the neural pathways are liberated from the burdens of confinement, when thought moves independently, unfettered by inner or outer chains. The more freely the thoughts travel, the freer the individual. And with each intellectual conquest, autonomy deepens. Yet the one who is not bound to anyone has surely volunteered for battle against the unknown, summoned by courage, or perhaps by recklessness. Either way, the inequality of courage among individuals suggests, unexpectedly, that freedom itself is relative. If all strive for liberty, but not all possess the same spiritual stamina, then freedom is not experienced equally. What is a mere path for one may be an expedition for another. A hill may feel like a mountain. A spring may appear as a river. A grove, a vast forest.

Insincerity with oneself breeds a subtle cowardice—one that refracts reality through a distorted mirror of fear. The human tendency to lack bravery creates an opening for society to implant ideological seeds deep within the psyche. And as a result, individuals begin to accept a mode of life shaped by ambient pressures. Freedom ceases to originate from within the mind; it is instead imported, externally modeled. Nothing standardized for all can be universally valid for the individual, not even freedom.

Take a trivial example: some view baldness as a minor flaw. If the individual accepts this notion as a personal deficiency, he surrenders autonomy by submitting to others' judgments. Worse still, he convinces himself of the inadequacy. But the one who dismisses it, who feels no discomfort, is the freer man, for he harbors no unnecessary disturbance. It is a simple metaphor, yes, but it scales infinitely in depth and hostility. The essence is this: Man cannot claim to be free while feasting on the banquet of borrowed beliefs.

The cruelest prison is born from the punishment of a darkened mind. Understandably so, any thought confined by freedom itself becomes more bearable. No room, no dream, no aspiration, no ideal is ever too small for the one who thinks freely. A person cannot be stripped of liberty when they hold absolute command over their thoughts. The most familiar image of captivity is the "prisoner." And yes, the haunting idea of being locked between four walls often acts as a silent enforcer of societal order, preventing certain transgressions. This fear serves a necessary role in civilization, for without it, structure would decay. Yet what remains absent from the collective conscience is a deeper truth: that a man imprisoned by law may possess a mind far more liberated than one who has never broken a single rule.

The person outside the bars, yet imprisoned within his own mind, lives with a muted hunger for life. To him, freedom becomes a burden, a weight without shape. He may have a large family, yet feel alone. He may purchase the house of his dreams, only to dwell in its nightmares. He may travel the world, yet each journey becomes a corridor of anxiety, his thoughts enslaved to the idea of returning home. Movement no longer frees him; it binds him.

Dark thoughts estrange a man from reality. Liberty transforms into a distant mirage, and every touch of the world becomes painful. It is a discipline of misfortune. The most tragic form of captivity is self-incarceration—a snare so cunning that even the strongest may fall prey to it. In this torment, a man who lives in a palace may feel the chill of his own walls more sharply than a beggar in the wind. A glance at the ceiling becomes a premonition of collapse. Climbing stairs exhausts him before his foot even touches the first step. Everything collapses inward.

Freedom bears a diagnosis: it is the ailment of the one who loves life. If the bipedal, rational, and articulate animal holds any true affection for living, then it has no alternative but to fall ill with freedom. Otherwise, love turns to hatred, joy dissolves into sorrow, peace vanishes and conflict arises, and beauty is deformed into ugliness. This infection does not take hold instinctively, it spreads consciously, through circumstantial experiences shaped by one's status and capabilities. These experiences are administered in differing doses from person to person, explaining why the germ of liberty does not flourish uniformly and why each individual describes and perceives its effects in their own way.

  The civic-minded citizen with modest life experience may define freedom as the act of voting and the license to curse leaders without consequence. But to be free is vastly more than that. As an aside, has insult become a virtue of independence? If so, many of society's ailments begin there, within the individual. The bachelor might equate liberty with the avoidance of responsibility. Marriage or the birth of a child may seem like sacrifices of freedom, and this discomfort of vision pushes him toward indefinite postponement of commitment. The peasant, on the other hand, sees liberty in a small plot of land, a few animals, a modest house, and a life in harmony with nature. His isolated, contained world soothes his hunger for independence. If this simplicity is indeed the truest form of freedom, then the wanderer, the man without fixed address, must be less free? Not quite. Only presumptively so.

The peasant represents a social extreme, mostly invisible in modern society, yet he occupies the foundational tier. The elite may dine well, but they do so thanks to him.

At the opposite end of the spectrum lies the wealthy man—for whom freedom becomes a vice of money.

Through thought, one must extrapolate the obstacle from the need. Ask a man what troubles him, and you'll uncover what separates him from independence. Freedom does not consist of fleeing restriction, but in accepting and renouncing the burden of limitation. No one escapes all constraint. And no one fully embodies the ideal of absolute freedom. Nature has never distributed rights, powers, or talents evenly. Hierarchy defines it.

Every conscious blockage narrows the circle of those in harmony with the universe. In the end, only those survive who have fully detached, while those clinging to everything dissolve. The only upward path passes through the bridge of the mind, as an inner reality. Negativity arises when the void stems not from the world outside, but from within ourselves.

It is tragic to admit: man might have been freer if one word were missing from his vocabulary: *freedom.* Why? Because without reason, animals dwell peacefully in the absence of discontent, restriction, or lack. They live without the tyranny of definition. But man cannot, because for him, boundaries stir unease.

If he were a fish, he would wish to fly.
If he were a butterfly, he would want to live longer.
If he were a tree, he would lament his immobility.
If he were an antelope, he would curse being prey.
If he were a stone, he would mourn the absence of love.
Reason itself stands at odds with the concept of liberty. How

can man act on his will or desire, when he constantly yearns for what he cannot have? Not always, but often. Be it an impossible love, an unreachable career, or an infinite fortune, he becomes prisoner to his own mind.

Worse still, he can become a perfect captive of attainable dreams—when he aspires to something within reach but makes no effort to pursue it. An idea without action turns liberty into a pendulum. One swings easily from the ecstasy of a dream to the despair of hesitation.

In these moments, one believes the idea will bring longed-for independence, but when they delay, that belief is replaced by anxiety. The cure comes in two forms: act—or let go.

Thus, sometimes even renunciation becomes an act of emancipation. Sometimes, surrendering a goal prepares the soul for joy. It may not be the best path—but it's better than the limbo of craving and inaction. Life moves in turns. There is always a better place than the one you stand in—even if it's not yet a great one. All that man must do is improve his position.

Stagnation compresses existence.

If obsession with something, whether impossible or merely possible, can offend the state of freedom, then the same can be said about indifference. When someone exhibits a lack of concern, not in isolated instances, but in a generalized, enduring way, they become enclosed in an endless mixture of boredom and desolation.

One cannot simultaneously manifest a passion for freedom and for the mundane. Perhaps not at the same time, but even slightly delayed, these two forces contradict one another. This isn't about reaching a *freedom of detachment*, but about finding joy *through attachment*. If a person feels a sharp boredom born from disinterest, then a life lived without interest persists in birthing a kind of absence—from dependency, from purpose.

Strangely enough, independence can suppress freedom if it brings unhappiness. Because the sorrowful are prisoners hired to serve discontent. They need fulfillment—attachments, or even dependencies—to be released. A person can be dependent on reading, yet that doesn't mean they've lost their freedom, it expands it. They might be dependent on work, and that doesn't diminish their autonomy, it intensifies it. Without being tied to something, man becomes untethered from meaning.

The essence of living, of being free, of loving, it all dissipates without joy anchored in a specific interest. Prolonged boredom locks a person outside the spectrum of existence.

Any genuine interest, whether in little, in much, or in everything, adds a note of purpose to one's life. And for this reason, the one who lacks concern ends up scorning every possible form of liberation from meaninglessness.

Usually, those who are funny, outwardly positive, often grew up in circumstances far from joyful, sometimes deeply tragic. By the same logic, those born into wide-ranging freedom are more prone to closing themselves off from society. It's a strange phenomenon, but it seems that no one remains unaffected by either lack or abundance. It's more likely for a person to instinctively detach from what they already have, while reaching toward what they lack—especially in the early stages of discovery.

By human nature, a child is born, begins to grow, to explore, and to learn. Along the way, they seek their place in life, and more often than not, they are drawn toward whatever is missing from their surroundings. This doesn't apply only to physical space, but also to ideologies, careers, or habits—often chosen to deviate from the familiar. For example, there are people who grow into adulthood with a deep aversion to alcohol, precisely because they were raised in families plagued by it. Or children who outright refuse to pursue their parents' professions. Of course, this isn't always the case, it's just a common tendency. The same applies to freedom. A child raised in a world of freedom finds that liberty becomes normalized, familiar, even mundane. It no longer holds the same sacred value as it might for someone who has known oppression.

In a world of openness, isolation begins to allure. In an extroverted society, the pull of introversion intensifies. This is not to say that introversion or solitude are inherently less "free" ways of living, but rather, it suggests that an overly open society can naturally seduce some into the intimacy of withdrawal.

Freedom takes root naturally and is ostentatiously improvised; innate and flamboyantly intertwined. A multitude of traits, some inherited, others developed intuitively, play a role in man's struggle against limitation. In his pursuit of freedom, he both leans on and stumbles over his natural instincts, which may serve him or betray him.

Two guardians, mutually hostile, watch over human existence: fear and courage. From the beginning of time to the present day, these two eternal sentries have shaped human life, disrupted its rhythm, and molded the course of history according to their degree of influence.

Fear is a kind of wisdom of inspiration, an instinctual awareness of danger. It serves as a compass, helping avoid tragedy. Without it, all of humanity would face risk with irrational defiance. Danger itself cannot be denied, it is real and concrete. Only perception can be distorted. Without a mechanism for anticipating misfortune, human vulnerability would be constantly exposed to the laws of nature. One person might survive by refusing to eat a mushroom out of fear, while another might perish by ignoring the same risk. But even that has its role in nature, someone must fall so that another may thrive.

In essence, then, fear is not inherently bad, it becomes dangerous only when the individual loses the ability to accurately assess risk. When fear exceeds what is reasonable.

When perception drifts into delusion. This is why humanity needed a counterbalance—a force to resist paralyzing dread. Otherwise, man would remain forever imprisoned by an anxiety over possible danger, whether real or imagined, trivial or life-threatening.

Courage gives rise to the freedom of action that paves the way to triumph. A master of fear becomes a competent servant of courage. As a popular saying goes, *"You receive what you serve."* Therefore, without boldness, success depletes itself early, and cowardice lingers far too long. Life pardons no scene of cowardice, just as fear permits no act of freedom. Naturally, everyone must conquer their fears in order to access the full richness of life. If they don't, resentment takes root.

Yet fear isn't always conquered by courage. Sometimes, it's replaced by a greater fear—the "bigger fish" principle. If a wanderer stumbles upon a wild beast, they may find leaping into a ravine or lake, the lesser danger, more acceptable, even hopeful, in contrast to being devoured. Likewise, in a more common example, people may overcome the fear of relationships out of an even deeper fear of loneliness. Ultimately, true courage surpasses all inner phantoms, especially the fear of ridicule, failure, rejection, or defeat. And often, all it takes is one second of bravery to dispel an eternity of hostility.

If a person doesn't look into the mirror for courage and confidence, they will not find them anywhere else. Not in the Sahara Desert, not in the middle of the Pacific Ocean, not on the mountain peaks. This isn't an invitation to narcissism, it is a call to personal accountability. One must strengthen their image in their own eyes, fortify themselves with the firm awareness that who they are today is not their final form. They must be demanding with themselves, because if not, others surely will be. Freedom begins by breaking loose from the one figure who most often traps us in contagious passivity: ourselves.

Awareness solves half the problem; the other half requires action. Independence is a dependency on self-conviction. After all, how can someone reach a state of freedom if they don't push themselves? Will anyone show up, take them by the hand, and ask: *"Would you like some freedom?"* Of course not. Every person must forge their own strange weapon to confront weakness. But, and this is crucial, they must not polish that weapon with too much admiration, affection, interest, or pleasure, or they risk creating something worse: a narcissist.

A narcissist is not just lost, he is dangerous. If he were the captain of a sinking ship, he'd freeze in awe of his own image. He would chase a fantasy of escape while leaving others to drown. It wouldn't be cowardice, it would be a lack of empathy, modesty, care, and responsibility. In truth, the narcissist is a prisoner of himself. He cannot be called free, he lacks many of the essential qualities that negate irrelevance and vague thinking.

Because true autonomy requires more than an extravagant alliance with one's inner self—it requires connection to the outside beyond.

Why do people, generally, believe that fear is inherently bad? Fear becomes detrimental only when it is accepted blindly or left unchallenged. In the spirit of change, and especially of progress, fear is the very condition that propels one beyond the immanent boundaries of mediocrity, for most inner revolutions begin precisely there. When someone confronts a fear, they either remain imprisoned by the mistake of letting fear dictate their existence, or they summon enough courage and trust to render that fear irrelevant. In doing so, they unlock behavioral innovation and experience a genuine liberation. He who carries many fears is a fortunate man, for he holds enough reasons to let go of his miseries.

Often, a fright becomes so intolerable that the individual decides to confront it—and, through that confrontation, rediscovers themselves in a renewed posture: stronger, wiser, more resilient. To be terrified by something is, in fact, an opportunity to unveil a better, more refined version of oneself, and a deeper sense of necessity in life. As an old proverb says: *"Need teaches."* Indeed, no one would succeed in gaining wisdom without first enduring confusion.

Could a human truly be human, without ever confusing confusion itself?

It would be no different than calling a lion a predator when all it does is tear at a carcass delivered in a cage. In every creature where fear lies dormant, a freedom also sleeps, awaiting its moment of becoming. The more fears one faces and overcomes, the more clearly defined their sense of liberty becomes—*for without fear, certain experiences would remain forever unknown.* Take, for example, a young person afraid of heights or vast open spaces. If they choose to hike through the mountains, their fear will begin to fade, and simultaneously, a new passion for nature may bloom. Or the individual terrified of public speaking who, by chance or will, ends up delivering a speech, handles it well, and receives praise—suddenly, they've gained confidence, and sometimes, even discovered a calling as a speaker.

The brain is drawn to challenges it manages to overcome. Once an obstacle is conquered, the mind shifts its label: from resentment to challenge, from burden to fuel.

Those bored with the ordinary often find meaning and joy in the very things that once repelled them. This is fear as potential passion. But there's also fear that comes from pressure, a demanding fear.

Psychologists around the world often discuss its most potent form: the fear of poverty.

Without this looming shadow, people might lack ambition or tolerance for discomfort, and instead surrender to complacency. Similarly, there's a comparative fear, when someone looks at another who suffers, who is broken by life's hardships, and asks: *"What must I do to avoid becoming like that?"* In conclusion, fear is not purely evil, nor a curse or sin—

it is a gift, waiting to be unwrapped, through which a stronger, more capable human being emerges.

In the contract of life, freedom is a clause; and when a person fails to honor it, they enter an indefinite existential furlough. To live without a meaningful form of independence is to be exiled into the realm of superficiality. It is clear: no one gravitates toward the trivial when vast possibilities are within reach, and no one feels compelled to refrain when drawn by greatness.

Limitations are like silent crimes against hope, self-inflicted in the absence of full autonomy. No individual could ever rise as an innovator, an explorer, or a conqueror while shackled by restraint. And equally, without having tasted freedom, one cannot awaken the appetite for transformation, at least not within a meaningful context.

Could a horse develop its gallop if confined to a stable?

Could a human embrace change while trapped in denial?

Freedom is like salt: essential in every preparation. Without it, all human creation would lack expression, bland at best, and in many cases, impossible. It follows naturally that where restriction dominates, opportunities are lost, human potential is dulled, and everything appears diluted into moderation. When independence is not prioritized, not pursued to fulfillment, life unfolds under the courteous mask of deficiency, a polite chaos filled with quiet disruptions.

Thus, freedom is not the only ingredient of existence—but it is one of the most essential.

Without it, the recipe of being lacks integrity, and the result is less than what it could have been. That is why freedom is an ingredient of pure existence, not the only one, but a deeply constitutive one.

4

Happiness

Unhappiness reveals itself as a pronounced vexation of the intelligent. It is the cruel fate of those who possess the capacity to discern, to filter thought and bring clarity into mind, or who are born with talent, that this very gift becomes the stumbling block that diverts them from the conquest of emotion. For lucidity acts as an antibody fighting to eliminate the hormone of happiness. Any dose of reason diminishes the intensity of joy, turning it from an elevated state to a mere calmness, with the same swiftness with which thoughts race through the mind. If joy were directly tethered to judgment, then the world would be an arid place, steeped in unbearable plenitude, in apocalyptic monotony—a permeable decay where happiness would become a rare feeling possessed only by the intellectually gifted.

The divine brilliance of separating happiness from rationality is a sacred denial of collective catastrophe, a necessary inequality for preserving spiritual balance, not merely individual, but societal. One of happiness's peculiar traits is that it can contaminate others, generously. Indeed, the most vivid form of emotional migration is seen between the conscious and the irrational: A dog wagging its tail at the sight of its master; An infant smiling when pampered by a parent; Or, in a dramatic scene, a person with severe impairment offering laughter and a radiant grin. All these are moments of happiness whose common denominator is the absence of lucidity and the effortless way their joy radiates outward.

If we were to imagine a world where happiness was directly correlated with intelligence, we'd be horrified. It would be a dystopia. It is, instead, an ideal gift that even the weak-minded, the inept, the irrational, the inarticulate—all breathe joy. In doing so, happiness becomes as widespread as air itself, it creates an agreeable atmosphere in our world. More often than not, the intelligent are bound to accept that their mission on this planet is not to directly contribute to the spiritual uplift of those around them through the mere offering of joy, comic performers and artists perhaps being rare exceptions.

A highly intelligent person with easy access to happiness would disturb the energetic equilibrium that sustains emotional order in society. Each individual, whether knowingly or not, contributes to the collective well-being. And a mind both highly skilled and frequently joyful would amount to a cosmic privilege, one that would feel unjust to those less endowed intellectually. Every person holds both lacks and strengths, and the filling of these voids can occur only through human connection.

When thought ignites, happiness dims. Why? Because everything seeks balance.

If a person were already warmed by joy, what incentive would remain to strike the spark of thought? Delight would consume their focus. But when one feels the chill and harshness of sorrow, the only way not to become numb—frozen in sadness—is to set the mind ablaze.

Could a philosopher truly be a philosopher if he burned with happiness?

In essence, the great minds of history were exiled from joy and cast into fates of introspective torment, sentenced to endlessly wander the realm of inner turmoil. The acceptance that happiness is elusive, especially for those tightly bound to reason and lucidity, is not only beneficial individually but also collectively. Refusing this truth would intensify the spiritual agony of the intelligent, pushing them toward despair, and away from creation, the very act that could lead to their fulfillment.

Creation seldom springs from joy, but almost merely an offspring of inner disquiet. The great minds of the world abandoned selfish pursuits when they made history, for no masterpiece, invention, scientific law, or cultural breakthrough has ever emerged from a simple desire to feel joy. Had the geniuses of the world been distracted by euphoria, the face of civilization would look utterly different. Rarely, if ever, has a work of art, a piece of music, a discovery, or a great invention sprung from an individual's yearning for happiness. More often, their work served as the necessary filler for a void left by the absence of joy. Their emptiness gave others joy.

What would life be without music, for example? Lifeless. If music had never existed, the funeral bell might have been the most spirited sound we knew. In principle, creation is born from an individual's desire to soothe the ache of sorrow— the struggle of eluding happiness. They seek refuge, a place to sort through thoughts, and their skill, longing, passion, and motivation become a catalyst, accelerating the brain's chemical reaction toward creation; until misfortune fades as a concern.

Unhappiness unleashed creation. Happiness birthed expressiveness. Both are needed to stir the extraordinary: One provokes the unusual. The other evokes wonder. First, there is the state of troubled existence, which bends the mind into a loop of deep reflection, a posture that curves perspective toward making. Then, in the moment of creation's lightning strike, joy arises, carrying expressive beauty into form.

The correlation between happiness and the biological nature of the human being is not the only thread that weaves through our emotional state, social status imposes its own pressure on the mind, reshaping perception and, with it, distorting reality itself. Indeed, this is one of the great risks of modern life: that external structures carve internal truths.

If liberty is not equal for all, peak happiness is—and both are deeply influenced by the social landscape. Within this dynamic, the essential distinction between freedom and joy lies in their relatability: freedom is subjective, happiness is universal. One may experience freedom on a different spectrum than another, but joy strikes with equal intensity, provided the stimulus aligns with each individual's social context. A hermit receiving new clothes may feel the same surge of joy as a professor buying a brand-new car.

Paradoxically, intellectual advancement and material success become the baggage that burdens the journey toward happiness. As one ascends the social or cognitive hierarchy, the ability to find joy in small, humble things begins to fade.

Simplicity is the most accessible mold from which the key to happiness is cast. Yet, life becomes increasingly convoluted, especially when the mind is trained with discipline, regularity, and ambition. In such cases, reverence for the rudimentary becomes diminished, even discarded.

Just as a bucket of water feels heavier to the frail than to the strong, both literally and metaphorically, so too do primitive experiences weigh more heavily in meaning for the unschooled than for the highly educated. Everyone needs simplicity. It is the hidden principle that balances divergent emotions and harmonizes the complex scales of life. Those obsessed with intellect are especially vulnerable to unhappiness when their heightened senses no longer respond to the beauty of simplicity.

Whether physical or intellectual, strength invites the instinctive betrayal of ease. Power, like sensitivity, must be summoned purposefully—it is not defined merely by its presence. Often, things are far simpler than they appear. Problems resolve more easily than anticipated. To overlook simplicity is not necessarily arrogance, it is the unconscious reflex of being perplexed by one's own complexity. Living a life haunted by complications is one way to conjure power through dependency. But one must remain lucid: not every solution requires strength; not every experience must be difficult. Physical and mental prowess can distort perception if untempered by the sublime clarity of simplicity. Otherwise, the individual risks losing direction, endlessly seeking intricate routes when the path was plain all along.

The unconsciousness of the only animal aware of its journey through life is, paradoxically, its tragic fate. Man lives with his eyes fixed on the destination, one he rarely knows, while neglecting the significance of the small, deliberate steps. Obsessed with shortcuts, he traverses blindly through every path, and his adventure through the unknown becomes a lump of clay shaped by the hands of chaos. This mental blockage, marked by a fixed idea of *arriving somewhere*, a restless pursuit of meaning, is most often seen in those marching steadily along the path of self-development. And in doing so, they diminish the value of the simple and the near.

Yet, sometimes there is *nothing* at the destination, and joy could have been found along the way. A trail may bloom with flowers, fruits, creatures, springs, or other splendors, while its end may offer only a barren, lifeless patch of dust.

If the experience of the journey holds more joy than its destination, then one might say: to attain things is a greater happiness that surpasses the one found in possession. The bitterness at the end is unjustified when fulfillment has quietly bloomed throughout the process. Every accomplishment is valuable in its own right; all that unfolds on the path toward a goal serves as an antidote to the obsession with ownership. If possession alone were the reason for existence, then every gain, every triumph, every achievement would reduce to a slow strangling of meaning. It is more exhilarating to build an empire than to govern it—for creation relies on vision, while governance is bound to responsibility.

From the enigma of life's unfolding emerges both panic and euphoria, twin sensations birthed by mystery and limitation. No one can have it all in a world where each soul wrestles with life through means of its own. All paths pass through beautiful stretches, but not all destinations offer a view worth seeing. Like a delirium of calculation, the probability of encountering beauty during the journey is high, while the certainty of finding it at the end remains elusive. Thus, the pursuit of a purpose bestows meaning, quenching the existential thirst for necessity while simultaneously saturating the soul with fulfillment. And so, pity is the only fitting sentiment toward those who inherit the success of others. For they have been denied the true joy that arises only through the courageous pursuit of small, personal victories.

A permanent state of well-being is like a storm for which everyone prepares, but which never truly arrives, because this tempest exists only in the vitality of imagination. Unending joy would stand as a sin of hope itself. What meaning would trust in the future still hold, if the present were already ideal? No one would linger in anticipation if desire no longer stemmed from a void to be filled. Happiness unfolds in fleeting moments, brief intervals scattered across life's stages. It cannot exist as an unbroken, sustained condition over time.

These short-lived impulses that ignite joy are not only brief, but they also fade in intensity with repetition. Unlike an animal, voiceless, instinctive, ever-joyful over the same experience, a human being experiences the apex of joy upon encountering something for the first time. With each repetition, the emotional intensity wanes until it settles into familiarity. This dissonance with repetition is the clearest signal of impending unhappiness.

What happens when a child receives a dog? In its short life, the animal will be overwhelmed with joy at each reunion with its young master. Meanwhile, the child delights excessively in those early weeks. But over time, without intending to, the joy softens into habit, until, finally, the pet's passing delivers a harsh lesson: the pain of loss through attachment.

A first kiss, first car, first paycheck, first home, first party, vacation, success, none can be relived with the same vigor. Humanity's great sorrow is that once it discovers an absolute pleasure, it cannot sustain it, nor replicate it. And since the brain cannot recreate the original high, it forges a dependency—one that edges dangerously close to vice.

The final drop that spills the cup of pleasure into bitterness is routine. This gradual descent from joy to emptiness, through the need to repeat certain habits, is the misfortune that drowns every spark of enthusiasm. Routine strangles all passion, causes life to lose its sense of significance, and hastens the sensation that time is slipping away. Memory no longer bothers to retain days that resemble each other, so they vanish. And when one later wonders where the time went, there is only silence. The burden of memories has an antidote: routine— and not only that, it also fills memory with emptiness.

Forgetfulness serves people so well that, in gratitude, they forge a pact with the brain: You help me erase the pain, and I promise to bring you joy. But in the end, no one upholds their end of the deal. And once the pact dissolves, everything is lost, either in a passion for monotony or, worse, in a habit of bitterness.

The mind embeds within one's consciousness a brutal truth: If you are incapable of storing good moments, you will be left with a collection of suffering, and I can no longer help you. In the absence of joy, all the voids, torments, and above all, the frenzy of emptiness, fill a person's inner world. And that world begins to revolve entirely around unhappiness.

Nothing seems more absurd than craving happiness. Every joy is internalized in its own peculiar way. And those who believe they have the privilege of sheltering it privately are mistaken. They end up gazing inward with self-doubt, turmoil, and torment, haunted by imagined impressions. When a person finally understands that happiness is not a prey to be hunted, but a predator that chooses its moment to strike, their perception of life shifts entirely. Everything we do in our daily routine is, at its core, a desperate attempt to extract meaning from existence. And this very attempt only deepens the disdain happiness often shows toward us. It would be far more effective to mask one's bitterness; for in doing so, one becomes far more enticing in the eyes of this sentimental colossus. Through positivity, kindness, contentment, small victories, simplicity, love, or anything that generates sincere satisfaction, a person prepares themselves as a feast that happiness will eventually devour. And it will. Conversely, through negativity, malice, hatred, or anything ugly, a person bait themselves into the claws of misery. In truth, every relationship in the world abides by the law of attraction, nothing can be forcibly united. And even our bond with joy is no exception to this rule. From this, one may subtly conclude: the pursuit of happiness is misguided. To entice it, through thoughts or deeds, is the surest way to receive it. In this light, it is far better to be pursued by happiness than to chase it.

In life, the joyful often wander into traps of their own making, while the miserable desperately seek escape. Everything seems to revolve around these snares, and man is nothing but a lab rat for the amusement of fate. People insert themselves, or withdraw, again and again, until one day they freeze, unable to bear it anymore. To persist, earnestly and without irony, in repeating a deceptive habit until it collapses, is, strangely, a commendable talent of unconscious endurance.

Those who subsist in happiness through foolish pleasures and hedonistic rituals deserve a certain admiration—for the ease with which they tread through life. But eventually, nearly all will be shaken by an unrelenting regret. No one can fully reconcile with the time wasted on whims.

What argument could be more persuasive in the war against gratitude for existence? Is it better to conquer life by the illusion of consistency, or to impose oneself through constant resignation to reality?

Strangely enough, it is not the real that helps one clear the fog from their eyes, it often blurs them further. Rather, it's the false, the sense that one's meaning might lie in trivialities, that occasionally brings clarity. One man who stretches distractions across the years convinces himself he has not lived in vain. Another, who shortens his pleasures under the weight of each moment, feels life is a constant waiting room.

Perhaps we are all foolish enough to bury our bitterness inside our own disappointments. But none of us can honestly claim to embrace the fading of the ridiculous. Everything becomes oddly theatrical when it meets the void.

Undeniably, the one who obsessively clings to happiness, stimulated daily through hedonism, will, as if by obligation, be gifted one final act of glory: regret. The day will come when, after countless artificial joys, they will ask themselves, "How did I waste so much time on indulgences?" At first, it seems delightful to seduce oneself with daily amusements. But in the end, the seduction turns humiliating. And for those who experience the pain born from pleasure, days of desolation are coming. Regret holds no falsehood, it is kept only of truth. If you lie to regret, it turns into resignation.

The same can be said of the one on the opposite end, the one who never stimulates joy, but rather, cultivates misery. The one who treats lucidity as naturally as breathing, who denies every small pleasure because, at the edge of reason, he sees everything as meaningless, except for some unreachable ideals. Life, through absolute illusion, composes itself in intemperance; through absolute reality, it decomposes into aspersion. Only through a mixture of the true and the imagined, can we navigate the full range of human experience. Through illusion, man collides with realities; through reality, he stumbles into illusions. Reality without unreality is as obscure as a fog-soaked night. Unreality without reality is as blinding as a blazing desert sun full of mirages.

According to merit and penalty — a principle faithfully upheld by all who exalt, perhaps excessively, a life of utility. Everyone is, at some point, punished by their own virtues when those virtues are employed, sometimes without discernment, for a subjective gain. So, what does man deserve more: happiness or suffering? He deserves only what he labors for. Both joy and sorrow are whims of a monopoly of fragmented thoughts, worn down by the fatigue of existing. No one would care about emotional states if they were exempt from the burden of existence. And likewise, no one would wander into joy or hardship unless such ventures were tied to usefulness. Give a child a toy, and he rejoices. Give him a book, and he grows irritable. Thus, emotional response is shaped by utilitarian criteria. From this, another insight emerges: amusement brings fleeting joy, while thought invites discomfort.

Habits are forged in childhood. Adults are merely children

who have swapped external stimuli for internal ones. When it comes to happiness, people preserve a consistent standard throughout life, formed in youth and silently recognized with age. If society teaches children to seek joy without reason, those children, as adults, will equate shallow pleasure with happiness and associate rational thought with distress. Almost reflexively so.

Intelligent people tend to carry more sorrow than those less gifted. They possess an additional faculty: the rational filter. Lucidity, in this context, is an aphrodisiac for sorrow; innocence, a lure for joy. Intelligence, utility, and pleasure, these three must be carefully considered, especially by those responsible for preparing the young for the future. A young person with intellectual capacity, accustomed to finding happiness in trivialities, may come to view his own intelligence as a hindrance to joy once he reaches maturity.

There is a limit to happiness: it cannot exist beyond the moment. Permanence traps joy, distancing it from the human being through a subtle aversion to intensity, while simultaneously expressing an objective sympathy for memory, where all happiness eventually resides. If time did not exist, joy would not dissolve into weeping delight. In its essence, happiness is an accomplishment bound to the present, a spark meant to rescue a weary life. That is why joy is best experienced through the isolation of feeling from duration. More precisely, happiness is an existential acceleration, a surge of adrenaline, not a constant stretched across time. Its passion speaks in immediacy.

Otherwise, time would smother happiness into a blend of projection and recollection. But time itself cannot do this, only the human mind can. When we push happiness into the future, we amplify anxiety; when we pull it from the past, we nurture nostalgia. This temporal displacement of joy is born from the luxury of thought. Indeed, spontaneity arises when thinking falters, when reflection dissolves in a fleeting mist, blurring clarity, for happiness is intimidated by reason. Without spontaneity, one is unfit for joy.

In the virtue of living, servitude to the moment becomes an ideal. Nothing rouses ecstasy more than a release from thought's heavy grip. The spontaneous are the ruffians of reason, gifted with a rare ability to succeed sorrow with humility. And what could be more tormenting than admiring a long, drawn-out joy in the absence of a sudden one? Perhaps it is the reverence for an eternal happiness, experienced under limited conditions. Spiritual satisfaction betrays time's authority, it defies it with abruptness, because it was never meant to last. Which raises an intriguing paradox: either happiness cannot exist in paradise, for paradise is eternal; or it does exist, but paradise is trapped in a perpetual present—locked in the moment.

Not only within the scope of time does joy show preference for the minute, it does so also within matter, revealing a reverence for the infinitesimal. One could argue that happiness has a kind of "megalophobia"—a fear of grandeur. Hypothetically, of course, since the clearest dimension of happiness perceptible to man is time. He can recall duration with ease, yet struggles to measure the intensity of lived experiences, or the weight of subtle impressions. What is undefined is often more intelligible to the human mind. It is a curse of sorts: the void appears more vast than matter itself.

In the canvas of life, joy is found in the details. Naturally, the joyful moments in life are details, tiny brushstrokes on a vast canvas. And the further one steps back to widen the perspective, the blurrier those details become. By implication, details only matter because they are precise; otherwise, they would be mere filler.

The one who finds no joy in walking will feel no true affection for the journey.

The one who does not crave a portion will grow tired of a feast.

The one unmoved by a single quote will be wearied by an entire book.

The one who cannot ignite a moment will extinguish the flow of time.

The one who finds no delight in small things will grow bored of everything.

The one who does not gain a friend will lose an entire circle.

The one who cannot admire a single flower will come to resent a garden.

The one who avoids unexpected fun will punish themselves with planned monotony.

Sooner or later, every person comes to recognize the value of the small. Grandiosity, when pursued obsessively, expels us from the string of subtle joys that make life feel fluid and bearable. Without them, the journey becomes disjointed, skipping from one hollow peak to another. Life flows through the minor; no one lives a fulfilled life by greatness alone. Within the maximum lies a minimum, but within the minimum, there is no maximum, it remains the same. Once one reaches the heights of aspiration, there often follows a humbling descent, a resignation thickened by disappointment. The mind, like a sieve, is shaped to filter happiness. And this sieve must be fine enough to catch the small, not just the grand. Otherwise, consciousness retains only the size, not the substance. Often, many small things, gathered together, outweigh a single great one. This does not mean smallness always surpasses greatness in meaning. But it should not be neglected. True joy lies in balance. Without it, the mind becomes polarized by scale, either lured by the vast or confined by the tiny, and happiness either stretches thin or collapses altogether. A man craving grandeur humbles essence, while one content with little diminishes purpose.

But that raises the enduring question: if balance is not achieved, which extreme better fosters happiness, the minimal or the maximal? Likely, it is the life aligned with small values. Simplicity is more accessible, more universal, more secure. And paradoxically, it may fill life's voids, sorrows, and shortcomings more abundantly than any grandeur ever could.

The absence of complications creates a quietude so deep, it silences planning altogether. Yet, when it comes to the inner state, joy or sorrow, such calm is far from impenetrable; it leaves the soul vulnerable to even the smallest disruptions. Momentary pleasures, accessible, common, and repetitive, do not fortify the spirit. On the contrary, they erode it gradually, almost irreversibly, through the vocation of dependency. Without intent, those addicted to comfort unwittingly reveal a borrowed suffering, drawn from the deceptive peace of stillness.

In essence, they validate a primal rule of nature: without exposure to danger, one cannot hope for complete resilience. Those who shun hardship remain impuissant in the face of calamity. How could one ever compel sorrow to retreat if all they seek is consequence-free happiness? Human nature, in its eccentric core, leans instinctively toward that which completes the sense of aliveness. A world without weight, without challenge, becomes a fragile bubble, easily shattered by adversity. Without risk, without pressure, without even a flicker of fear or thrill, a person drifts aimlessly through their own existence; tentative, unanchored. True exhilaration arises only from extravagance. And so, fascination with the extraordinary becomes the precursor to extraordinary joy.

There is no satisfaction like the one earned through a risk taken, especially when it turns victorious. That variety of happiness is rare, almost unrepeatable. Risk, by nature, teeters on the edge of potential danger, and that "potential" is precisely what imbues it with mystery and emotional gravity. Certainty dulls the vibrancy of emotions perfectly; it is one of those paradoxes where perfection ceases to be ideal, it becomes flaw.

Of course, risk also carries the probability of failure, and failure often materializes. It scares people away. But one of life's great achievements is learning to identify with loss just as one does with success. For if a risk doesn't cost everything, then something is always gained. As long as failure doesn't end the war, it will, eventually, deliver its reward: lessons, resilience, evolution, and ultimately, triumph.

Thus, the battle against sadness can be won not by avoidance, but through bold and extravagant confrontations—often the most exhilarating experiences a person can live. It requires a blend of thought, courage, dedication, and a measured dose of madness. That deliberate madness, the audacity to gamble with risk, assists the human spirit in humbling reality. And what would life be without the humiliation of reality? Nothing would remain but a descent into hopelessness, a detachment from all enthusiasm.

5

Love

What Is Love to a Human Being? What is love, if not the drop of water sliding down a blade of grass, the ray of sunlight scorching the petals of a flower, the spoonful of soil that covers a seed, the breeze that carries pollen? What is it, if not what time is to eternity, or matter to nature? Love is nothing less, and nothing more, than everything a person needs. It is the chaotic force that brings harmony to the soul, the infinity that fills the gap, the grace of conflict, the brilliance blindly pursued. It is a limited eternity, a tangible ideal.

It is the light that darkens thought, the dream that keeps you awake, the courage to live with the fear of loss, the joy of sharing what you receive, the eternal lived through fleeting instants, the discovery of what was never sought, the boundless bound, the flame that burns without scorch, the closeness of distance, the logicless reason, the fabricated truth, the brutal happiness—all gathered into one singular essence: Love.

LOVE

Love may be the one true disruption in nature's coherence. The only coherent thing about love is that its climax ends at the beginning.

The most beautiful feeling the universe has to offer does not abide by the universe's laws and cannot be sustained indefinitely through pragmatic flavor. On the contrary, it is the taste of love that makes reality digestible. Without it, life would be devoid of appetite, and madness would be the only thing on the menu.

The place of a human in the cosmos is always distant from their own presence. Wherever one feels most at ease, they are also the most misplaced. Every chosen place, every settled home renders the individual a long-gone stranger to themselves. What remains is a borrowed personality, a ghost of character inhabiting the inner space, not driven by exploration but by assimilation. The environment molds each person into a discoverer of the already-known: a replica placed gently within the collective mimicry of meaning.

Only at home, and only in solitude, does a person find a space truly their own, a realm untouched by the viral detachment from originality. Yet even this immunity from societal blending breeds its own affliction: despair. Solitude and home are ravaging lucidities, sanctuaries where the triumph of reason begins the excavation of self from revelation. Home is the only place where one may encounter both extremes found throughout existence: either love, or madness. Which is why, if humans had not been granted a space of their own, they would never have conceived these two most defiant answers to reality. But in combination, over long spans of time, solitude at home becomes catastrophic—because it forces confrontation with truth too piercing to endure. One cannot dwell too long near perceptible reality without clinging to the one exception to the horror of unfiltered awareness: love.

What has man done to deserve such an exemption from the concrete? Nothing. Can nature be accused of pity, of favoritism toward the human race? Not in the least. Since the dawn of time, humanity has shown relentless perseverance in its struggle with existence. It has not stood idle, indifferent. It has fought—tirelessly, fervently—for whatever it believed in. And, across the ages, love has emerged as the model par excellence, the supreme form of liberation from the chains of reality. The yearning of every person to walk the Earth has marched, without deviation, toward this singular hope. Every personal void was filled with gestures of friendship. Every unending pain found its terminus in love. All shared misfortune was gathered and softened in the warmth of affection. Love has been, and perhaps still is, the only ideal that has remained loyally beside humanity since its beginnings, enduring unshaken through centuries, immune to the erosion of time or cultural decay.

People often place "love" and "conquest" side by side, because within the depths of their unconscious lingers an ideological seed, planted by ancestors who long ago came to believe that love is not warfare, but rather, the most powerful weapon man possesses in his battle with life. This inheritance passed from generation to generation, standing as a gateway to emotional solace when, in the darkest of days, nothing else could pacify the soul's unrest.

History has been brutal. Rich in atrocities. And love was the response.

It summoned peace in times of war.

It stood in place of food during famine.

It united the isolated.

It was the balm that soothed disease.

The dream that lulled loneliness to sleep.

The cry that comforted longing.

Nothing more, yet nothing less, than fragments of eternity made momentary.

Love was. Love is. But will it be? If the theory is true that mankind created and nurtured this supreme feeling as a countermeasure to its cruel fate, a life steeped in hardship, suffering, and existential dread, then the reverse must also hold weight. If struggle fades, if hardship disappears, then so too might humanity's desperate need for love. The risk is that the comfort and the wellbeing might dull the hunger for inner solace. The soul may be distracted, enticed by abundance. Priorities will shift. The pleasure of living will be anchored more in the tangible than the transcendent. And this, the loss of spiritual yearning, may be, for the common soul, the most insidious punishment of all. A descent from a world that once revered the soul's silent hunger into one cursed by the hollow practicality of everything it contains.

The tension between the spiritual and the material is not merely abstract, it translates, palpably, into the lived experience of every individual, shaping the delicate architecture of mental equilibrium. A life devoid of spirituality tends to elevate even the most trivial possessions to a place of exaggerated worth. Conversely, a life stripped of material footing breeds a disconnection from progress itself.

In the human imagination, perfect love arises at the intersection of abstract devotion and physical intimacy. But in a world saturated by comfort and ease, the highest form of affection risks erosion, its significance diluted, its expression narrowed to mere instinct. When spirit is severed from love, affection devolves into biology; humanity recedes into animality.

Imagine, if you will, a thought experiment—science fiction in tone, but piercingly philosophical in implication: Two spacecraft are sent adrift into the vastness of the cosmos, populated by large groups of people. These travelers have no memory, no history, no connection to Earth or to each other. Communication between the vessels is impossible. They must begin again learning, discovering, constructing their world from a void.

In the first ship, life is dictated by an oppressive regime. Food is scarce, comfort is denied, freedom is restricted, culture is stifled, and labor is excessive. In the second ship, everything is abundant; food, hygiene, luxury, pleasure, freedom. Time is squandered with ease; leisure is limitless.

What becomes of love in each of these worlds, as centuries pass? Within the harsh confines of the first vessel, love becomes necessity. Affection arises early, out of need, out of the desperation to connect, to find meaning in shared suffering. These individuals, exposed to cruelty and deprivation, develop deeper, more soulful bonds. They are less utilitarian, more emotional, and far more attuned to goodness. The external absence of love gives rise to its internal generation—humans offer what the world withholds.

In such a setting, love becomes resistance. Its warmth defies cold conditions. Its persistence becomes protest. Drop by drop, emotional solidarity builds, until it surges, a tidal wave of sentiment strong enough to fracture the oppressive machinery of control. No tyrannical regime, no matter how unrelenting, can withstand the silent revolution of affection. Because, in the end, no social or personal upheaval has ever begun with greater force than love. Ultimately, no revolution, whether inner or social, has any other stirring surrogate but love.

On the other ship, the vessel of pleasure, things are different. In this world of abundance, people lean toward selfishness, mental lethargy, and spiritual erosion. Love becomes less a matter of emotional complementarity, more a physiological urge. Their emotional depth weakens wherever the mind is too busy being entertained, and deepens only where it seeks escape from oppression.

For love, at its core, is the madness of embracing suffering without discernment, and equally, the wisdom of pursuing joy with purpose. Without conscious love, the human being becomes merely a prisoner of life's instinctive exile. Whether it brings peace in torment or a pact with pleasure, love is always present, not betraying, as thought never abandons the idea it carries.

How do we find love in today's world? Looking at widely circulated statistics, some viral, some dubious, some telling, we glimpse an evolving trend: a growing number of women projected to remain single and childless; men increasingly disinterested in dating; divorce rates continuing to climb. These generalizations can't fully define the shape of love in our time, it would be naive to jump to conclusions, but they suggest one thing: love is becoming rarer.

The world is shifting. Standards of living are transforming, entertainment and opportunity flood daily life, time itself seems distorted. The individual is besieged by illusion. Unable to filter the barrage, he gets lost in a world too small for aspirations too large. Thus, existence becomes a spirit weighed down by malformed desires, unrealistic expectations, and a constant demand for more than what one deserves. He thinks outside his reach, devotes himself to arriving somewhere, yet never knows where, and, ultimately, collapses into the despair of a wasted life. In such conditions, love withers, hunted down by superficial criteria.

The tragedy of the lover is his inability to separate love's madness from the madness of reality. Life offers more propulsion to those who live in order to love, than to those who love merely in order to live. And life, spoiled and proud, like a stubborn child, often meets desperation with disdain, ignoring the pleas of those who beg for meaning, yet silently nurturing those attuned to affection. There lies a conflict of interest: life's tendency to inflict struggle, and humanity's yearning for solace. No path is laid out clear. Obstacles abound. Those who seek love through extravagance will not find it. Without struggle, intention remains just that, an eternal missed chance. In the end, life only offers one abstract gift: The satisfaction of having earned something truly deserved.

Can two people still love each other when everything around them changes? Can two people live the same emotions, with equal depth and intensity, if placed in radically different settings? What if they were moved from the city to the countryside, from the mountains to an island, from luxury into a shack? What if they fell from wealth to poverty, from careers to simplicity, from success to failure? What if their appearances changed, from overweight to thin, from immaculate clothes to rags, from eloquent speech to illiteracy?

Could lovers preserve their spiritual bond if the concrete reality around them shifted completely? Probably not. Probably yes, if the relationship is predestined. But more likely not, since with each change, the way one thinks will also change, and consequently, perception adjusts subjectively. And when one thinks too much, clarity is obscured by incoherence. Without objectivity, self-respect, and a steady self-image, a person becomes reckless in decisions, self-sabotages preferences, and ends up turning their own thinking into a wound that pushes love away rather than drawing it closer.

There are many who do not know their place in the world, they overestimate themselves and aim beyond their reach, presenting themselves as prizes to be won. Yet no one falls in love with a trophy. If they did, no one would ever pull the trigger, emotionally speaking. Choices become smothered by numbers.

Imagine a small settlement with an equal number of men and women, an ideal mathematical setup. Even there, romantic pairings unfold in a tangled way. A world void of loneliness remains a near impossibility. Most women would gravitate toward a narrow group of men, and those men would compete for the most desirable women. What remains are disappointed women who weren't chosen and an equal number of men who never entered the game. From those leftovers, conjunctural couples form; pairings made not from first choice, but from circumstance. Which means that most relationships are born from compromise rather than model. And so, not even in love does life grant people their most modest dream: To be with someone they truly and deeply desire. Those who reject this reality often find themselves on the lonely path.

In general, lonely people are more easily seduced by kindness, not because solitude is a virtue, but because they've had fewer opportunities to develop negative behaviors. Envy, jealousy, quarrels, conflict, hatred, anger, resentment—all require at least two people. Logically. Also, how many have realized they treat strangers better than their own family? No one behaves poorly with someone they just met, or have only known briefly. A man sits at a table, smiling politely at the waitress while scolding his wife across from him. A parent harshly yanks their child, yet treats their friend with calmness and gentleness. A child speaks respectfully to an elderly stranger but mocks and snaps at their own grandmother sitting nearby. Why?

Everyone should offer their best to their family, not to strangers. And yet, loved ones often become the most accessible dumping ground for all negative emotions. When someone feels more at ease with strangers than with their own, it leaves a bitter taste. Familiarity brings not only comfort, but also toxicity, anger, stress, anxiety, and injustice. A large family can be a blessing, but it may also come packaged with deep suffering. Paradoxically, family wants the best for us, yet often causes the most harm, intentionally or not.

By contrast, solitude is harsh, dark, and only a confused mind can endure it for long, everyone else eventually loses their grip on reality. Family is for everyone. But only the strong or indifferent manage to avoid the pitfalls it inevitably brings.

A flea without a dog is the purest form of solitude. For humans, loneliness is the only marriage guaranteed by a blind date. Nothing and no one can change a person more than their own self. Handing your fate over to yourself is a double-edged sword, it can sharpen you for success, or split you apart toward failure. Everyone makes that choice. Yet the sting of a victory earned by sacrificing love is agonizingly bitter. No one finds peace when tormented by the thought that love was just an obstacle to achievement. Living this way is only tolerable through acceptance. Solitude becomes the only truce before the argument even starts. The danger of going it alone is not just the risk of failing at life entirely, it also lies in the trap of dependency that follows the illusion of self-contained peace or happiness. Once accepted and adjusted to, solitude becomes incredibly hard to break away from. Any nostalgia for solitude becomes a remorse exiled from assent.

Some choose solitude because they love too much. They understand love beyond need. They carry it into a realm untouched by use or purpose, an abstract place, where reality is omitted, imagination overflows, and the sole aim is to conceive a perfect kind of love. Within every lonely romantic dwells an erotic spirit, a zealous romanticism, a poetic shyness, and not least, a dormant passion and a dreamlike longing. If they cannot live love in the concrete, they refine it internally. This is natural, human. For in the absence of experience, the tendency arises to strive toward perfection. Only when love is tested, does man come to terms with its imperfection. And as long as he dreams of it alone, he will sculpt it so finely in his mind that it becomes the very image of the absolute ideal. It will be difficult for him to find compatibility in real life, but should he find it, that love will be one drawn from fairy tales.

In truth, every great love story in history has begun after a melancholic solitude. For the one who has suffered long in longing, when they finally encounter love, they will layer the magnificent over the mere experience.

Then, there are others, those who, strangely enough, believe in "self-love." But self-love is a sentimental slander. Affection exists between two beings who commit to a shared ideal, who split and collect moments, who tumble through emotion, and who ultimately present, before the passage of time, the most effective defiance against it: love. To "love yourself" makes no sense. Quite the opposite, it is a kind of disorientation, especially when love implies fighting to fill what is missing within. Love is a battle of boldness and selflessness. Make no mistake: man's weakness is his strength to live alone. His strength is his weakness in the face of love. The bridge that links solitude and love is called the fear of living them. The bridge that connects fear and pleasure is the courage to confront them. The state of boldness is the history of fears passed.

Many, perhaps the majority, do not live a true love, but an illusion. The human brain is not designed to interpret reality objectively. It is, rather, a magnificent deceiver, one that helps us survive. It searches for evidence, sometimes even fabricates it, to support the narrative that circulates through our thoughts. It can be a loyal ally, helping you conquer unconditional good,

or a ruthless adversary that sabotages your very existence. Thus, the one who has solidified the idea that life is ugly, will be invaded by proof to support that claim, just as someone convinced that life is beautiful will find beauty everywhere. Prejudice is sturdier than reality itself. To put it differently, one may objectively have a good life, but if corrupted thoughts run through the mind, that life may be subjectively experienced as cruel. Prejudice may be tougher than a mountain, but it has a weakness: it moves slower than attraction.

When someone becomes emotionally attached to a person or a thing, counterarguments enter the mind with great difficulty, almost not at all. The same happens with feelings, emotions, and states of mind. The brain forges illusions, hopes, conspiracies, preconceptions, preferences, anything that upholds the thesis of a particular chapter in life. Without self awareness, perceptions easily slip into falsehood. Even love. This is why encounters that drift away from objectivity can't be trusted. They are not anchored in sincerity, but rather revolve around performance and pretense. Those who love with objectivity, with true passion, do not love to fool life, they love to save it.

Love at first sight is the purest, most truthful kind. It is undeniably real. In that moment, the mind is caught off guard, and has no time to analyze or dissect. Only when reality astonishes does the mind grow drowsy—it puts intervention to rest.

And in the far corner, where false love thrives, is digital affection: love encountered through technology, where energy, warmth, personality, and spirit fail to flow. There, only practical elements circulate, a multitude of conversations revolving around tangibles, and very few around emotion. It becomes a psychological game: an effort to convince the other person that you are exactly what they seek, a game that may, in the end, deceive both parties.

In truth, love seeks nothing. It is a journey with no destination, an insatiable itinerary. All that matters is a path unbroken by illusion, a procession of countless steps in harmony with the genuine. Only this way, at the end of love, we are greeted by the one regret that reconciles us with ourselves: the regret of suffering. Every love concludes with a regret, one that alters the value of time, and that is the most essential transformation. The regret of having stayed beside the wrong person, the seething confusion of having loved someone unworthy, this is the residue of an unreal connection. Wasted time becomes a reckless persecution within a fleeting life. But the regret of losing a true other half, that pain testifies to the depth, the truth, and to how sacred the time spent together really was. Life must be intoxicated by the spirit of beauty and authenticity. And maybe, just maybe, the only solution is to learn to love more discerningly: to no longer be drawn to superficial traits, deceived by fleeting perception or frightened by solitude; to stop rushing in without certainty. And so, after a long and noble struggle, we may finally grasp the meaning of love—and its profound contribution to our undeniable existence.

6

Success

There exists another obsession rooted in the collective consciousness, but one that, by no means, can be interpreted as an ideal. It is instead a phenomenon tied to the favorable made concrete. Its name is success. The ideal represents a tendency toward perfection, while success is the state reached after surpassing a particular form of personal disaster. Success is the point of balance, the middle ground between catastrophe and the ideal. A hammer may be considered the ideal tool for a nail; success would be managing to drive it in with a stone, while disaster would be having nothing at all, trying with bare hands. It would be absurd to present the act of hammering a nail with a hammer as success, as it's already considered a perfect act—devoid of challenge or uncertainty. Or, in a more abstract sense, freedom is an ideal for man, success is liberation from a specific fear, and disaster is remaining imprisoned by dread.

Many desire it, few seek it, even fewer find it, and barely a handful manage to maintain it. The order and disorder of society are constantly shaken by man's inability to resolve the equation of success. If the ideal is independent of the human being, an absolute measure, a virtual goal always just out of reach, and if nearly nothing in this world is definitively ideal but only presumed to be so, then success emerged from humanity's need to solidify empirical evolution, especially on a personal level. What breath would life have left if man were to eternally chase what cannot be attained—perfection? He would only breathe out the air of despair born of the unattainable.

Success can only be confirmed through comparison; it cannot exist inoperative. Everything is relational. At the same time, the world is extremely competitive, with many participants and only partially observed rules. The stench that perfumes the crowd is the reek of dishonest success. A seeker of truth cannot find peace in a world that has prospered through deceit and conflict. But neither can he afford to despair. For man, hope is, in its essence, what fragrance is to a butterfly: the impulse that draws him to his destination while others wander in the meadow. The loss of hope is to success what indolence is to hardship. Is there hope for humanity? No, perhaps only at the end. Is there hope for the individual? Yes, certainly, at the beginning.

Indeed, humanity is far from honorable, unworthy of collective praise, morally ill, and teeming with cheaters, but resignation is merely a psychological reflex born from seductive cowardice. To give up is not to be defeated by the lies others practice, but by the untapped truth within oneself. It is the suppression of enthusiasm, the modesty of ambition, that carries the honest person toward triumph. The onlooker to courage tends to believe the world is a place conquered by misfortune, sterile of virtue, and tirelessly resistant to the influence of good. Nothing could be more false. The coward is the hero who conquers defeat before ever entering the battle for honor. We cannot know when time will end, but we can be certain that the struggle between good and evil will endure for eternity. And if ever there is a victor, then time itself will consume its final drop. Until that moment, the spring of hope will not run dry; the righteous will rise in courage, and their victories will echo louder as the ranks of the deceitful swell.

The world is admirably constructed, with both good and evil. Everything exists in balance, disequilibrium is not a preference of nature but a counterweight, lest all collapse. When the army of the wicked grows, the virtuous will grow stronger. Temptation and admiration for deceit are the ingredients that drag individuals into the pitfall syndrome. And although success may come swiftly to those who cheat, it will not last. The price will be higher, and, more importantly, cheaters will eventually compete among themselves. The contest in dishonesty is fierce, only the truly unremarkable abstain. Yet, success earned through the courage to remain honest will be rewarded in kind: enduring through time, spared of ruthless competition, and free of ruinous costs.

A similar truth applies to the success pursued through intellect. It is by no means reserved for the most gifted; rather, it is conditioned by the direction of one's thoughts, not their depth. Remarkable achievement can be found at any rung of the intellectual ladder. The difference lies in who one meets on the steps. A fool thrives when surrounded by greater fools; while the wise elevate themselves through those wiser than him. Otherwise, neither would fully utilize their potential. And if the world appears to be a place where the inept succeed more often, it is perhaps because they are more widespread, and it is simply easier to advance among them.

Man is fragile, and defeat comes easily to him—even success can overwhelm. No one should pursue triumph before achieving personal growth. Victory, in the absence of a fortified character, may well signal one's undoing, whether that means the loss of one's mind, friends, family, or in the direst cases, life itself. The absurdity of fate reveals itself when a person becomes their own victim. Society offers more than enough examples of individuals who lose their way, follow misdirected paths, place their faith in confusion, and make a stop at powerlust or addiction on the road to ruin.

If the failed man clings to addiction to escape a life that offers him nothing, the successful man often abuses his fortune because he believes life has nothing left to surprise him with. Both are driven to the same verdict: an urge to escape reality. To liberate oneself from reality is to align with the denial of mystery. As long as curiosity stirs for what is unknown and unexplored, the temptation to detach from reality lies dormant. Without curiosity, man would have lacked the teacher needed to become human.

Unlike the defeated, who lack power and thus cannot misuse it, the accomplished individual becomes a societal threat when he fails to control the influence he holds. Nothing is more dangerously corrupt than a strong man with a weak spirit. The silent cry of history reminds us that empires have crumbled when fragile minds were seated on thrones; an enduring truth that proves the heights of success can be reached by the unworthy, but not endured by them. Like an animal raised in captivity, unable to survive in the wild, the person who stumbles into success, accidentally, effortlessly, or through inheritance, without deep personal cultivation, becomes a threat not only to his own autonomy but to the balance around him.

Human frailty is most visibly strained along the path to achievement. Success is not easily managed, and its continuation does not forgive fatigue. Man tires quickly of victory but never of loss. Born into failure, it is his hunger for triumph that elevates him into a semblance of the superhuman. No one perishes from failure—each bears an innate symbiosis with it. A man is rarely moved by a setback, for emotion belongs to achievement.

The only time failure stirs the soul is when it follows the taste of victory. That intense joy, that overwhelming release, sometimes even tears, that arrives with a great success is not random: it is the mind unloading all that it has borne through the journey. Labor, pain, sacrifice, determination, ambition, and devotion are the burdens of the victor. The defeated, by contrast, bears nothing, only the condition he was born into.

Thus, in the absence of personal investment, a man can go on losing indefinitely without ever screaming in despair that he's had enough. But success, true earned success, does not materialize out of nothing. It requires a goal, a direction, and the sacrifice of effort. That alone makes it harder to bear than failure. In the world we inhabit, it is exhausting to be someone, and comfortable to be no one. Emptiness favors relaxation; content demands strain.

The misfortune that holds man in darkness is called weakness. Without struggle, and without its defeat, no one can step into the light. There are moments when an individual may win a battle, but not the war, when he touches victory, only to swiftly collapse again into the abyss of failure. The strength of his own lack of strength drags him back. Those who walk from success to success are worthy of deep reverence, for they have conquered the human condition, and their mindset floats above mere chance. Yet calamity has many disguises that sabotage achievement. Perhaps the most insidious of them is comfort.

Comfort is the best vaccine against success. The disdain for the sickness bred in convenience is a necessary antidote to the temptation of a life left unfulfilled. Stillness breeds complacency and dulls the blade of ambition. No one marches into battle from a place of ease—it would be madness, a betrayal of judgment. All who fight for purpose do so only after surrendering comfort in a moment of necessary violence.

A man's life is like a snowball: growing only as it rolls. The human winter is suffering, and pain is the snow that binds it. Every step taken through struggle adds to his mass, his power. What matters is that he does not cling to pain, if his foot adheres too long, it freezes, and he remains trapped in suffering. A life without hardship leads nowhere. Easy things exist for rest; their place is before and after what is difficult. The journey of life is not linear but sinusoidal—an undulating path from good to bad, from ease to burden.

Lingering in pleasure has nothing to do with success. It is a mirage of fulfillment that leads all into irrelevance, like breath vanishing into fog. The pursuit of success in an atmosphere of comfort is a silent pact with disappointment, just as futile as the desire for distinction without competition. True striving needs resistance, a visible antagonist. Without it, ambition turns into apathy, a contract signed in the absence of adversity.

SUCCESS

The cage is a nest of comfort. Pigeons raised in a coop develop an irreversible attachment to that place—safety, food, water, companionship, and mating conditions imprint upon the bird a sense of "home." The pigeon becomes incapable of detachment from the familiar; it remains devout to the idea of the "well-known." Any distance triggers an acute longing to return.

The very thought of flight unsettles the human being. As a result, he clips his own wings, not out of caution for safety, but in pursuit of quietude. His house becomes his cage, willingly. Each day spent in comfort chips away at the altitude of his unrealized potential. No one reaches the summit of vitality after sinking into stagnation. Naturally, conquest is forged through struggle, not peace. The modern human is disinclined toward conflict, protest, or confrontation; he has become largely avoidant. A soft, non combative character, incapable even of regulating internal turmoil, and who, as a broader weight, finds difficulty in commanding even the smallest, most ordinary decisions.

How can anyone attain success in a fiercely competitive world if he cannot decisively and swiftly resolve a basic choice? Some people are paralyzed by a reflexive dithering, faced with a barren day and a few fruitful minutes, they'd rather satisfy the denial of growth. A blossoming perspective is worthy of communion—the butterfly teaches us this.

A life that leaves no trace is the insolence of sealing shut the path of time. Periods marked by historical voids are the offspring of societies that have drifted away from progress. History cannot exist without memory, and memory retains only the events. When people are imprisoned in comfort, decline and collapse become inevitable, no one is concerned with building; all are consumed by ease. No fool wishes to escape from goodness, and yet, despite his will, everything that begins must also end. Nature is structured with progression at its core, founded upon an essential mechanism called evolution. It is immune to extinction by virtue of its cyclical renewal—what is new replaces what is old. Man cannot defy this. If he could, our present world would not exist; progress would have halted at the first age of abundance. Humanity slips into the curse of regression when well-being becomes universally accessible, and the naivety of those who settle into such states without affirming the necessity to desire more becomes a silent condemnation upon generations yet to come. Greed arises when one desires the same thing repeatedly, not when one longs for what they have never had. Hunger for the new is what nourishes development.

Man can ignore, but not deny, aspects inherent to his existential reality. One of them is the fact that, in times of comfort, he becomes lazy and less creative, while in hardship, he turns inventive and industrious. Take a man and leave him alone on a deserted island—his need to survive will transform him into an ingenious being. He will build shelter, devise hunting strategies, experiment with basic agriculture, and invent clever ways to sustain himself. That same individual, placed in a setting of comfort where danger is minimal or nonexistent, will no longer be as capable or resourceful. He who makes peace with convenience begins a war with initiative. Stepping away from comfort is the battle begun yesterday, the defeat of today for the victory of tomorrow.

Inevitably, good precedes ill, and the man lulled by pleasure seldom senses the threat that looms. There may be no rational objection to a quiet life on a couch, a cozy home, a satisfactory job, unrestricted entertainment, and few material lacks, were it not for the slow creep of complacency, decay, and boredom. After all, no one is obliged or inherently indebted to contribute to society, yet a life of sustained ease turns on itself and becomes harmful to one's descendants. A life lived in the spirit of dopamine stimulation consecrates itself to anonymity, an existence void of great acts, detached from one's potential, a risk to personal fulfillment, and ultimately, a danger to collective progress. Once respect for the superficial is consolidated, remarkable constructions stand on shaky ground.

Humans are at their most effective and inventive when pressed by hardship, just as they become more wasteful and indulgent when immersed in comfort. The social system built upon repetitive labor has spawned the age of consumerism, which has rapidly accelerated the depletion of resources, while simultaneously stalling reform and temperance. The reason is simple: under the shelter of well-being, the brain ceases to optimize time for creation and becomes preoccupied with managing moments of pleasure. Clearly, when consumption hijacks the mind, production is no longer its focus. Success does not emerge from a mind enchanted by distraction. How many of the artists, inventors, physicists, or writers who etched their mark into history would have done so if they had lived by today's standards? Genius may not have been silenced entirely—but some would have remained unknown, perhaps.

A society that offers its citizens an accessible and abundant standard of living is, by definition, stable, enduring, and pacifistic. Yet, such a system significantly curtails the potential for personal development. It flattens mediocrity and encourages a chaotic exploitation of both physical and intellectual resources. Civilization, as a whole, relies on countless individual triumphs to propel the progress of humanity. Evolution will not be halted by any political or social system, there will always be those stubborn enough to go against the tide, but it will be slowed, and the distant future endangered, if the collective goal becomes nothing more than pleasure and consumption. Everyone needs an objective to find within themselves the argument for achievement, whether that objective is real or illusory, genuine or contrived, tested or theoretical. It is that aim which stirs the awakening toward change. Without it, all remains unchanged. The ambition that deceives the modern human lies in the love of luxury.

How absurdly easy it is to compete with the masses, and how imposing it is to compete with oneself. At the collective level, within social structures, competition becomes a servile debt to the ordinary, one devoid of any organic disillusionment with false knowledge. Paradoxically, while life appears to unfold as a rivalry with others, it ultimately reduces itself to a singular and solitary pursuit: personal victory. To succeed in asserting oneself in the world, regardless of the forms that assertion takes, is not a demonstration of universal mastery but rather a testimony to one's personal coherence. This suggests that humanity functions largely by artificial logic, because a truly natural concept would never house within it something inherently easy. People lack a collective awareness of the commonality between them, and this absence paves the way for an unrestrained descent into mediocrity.

That is why competition with the masses is revealed in its lowest common denominators: it is anything but complicated, on the contrary, it is painfully simple. Through an almost trivial skill, one individual can surpass millions who lack it. Tying one's shoes, boiling an egg—these are rudimentary tasks, yet not universally mastered. Or consider literacy: who believes reading and writing are complex skills? And yet those who possess them command a tool that eludes countless others. A person who reads just one hour a day refines their thinking to a level that quietly eclipses nearly all those who drift through existence carried by futility—in essence, nearly all of society.

And yet, a personal competition is anything but futile. It is arduous, meritorious, principled, integral to a structured life, and most importantly, it embodies the very vibration of the most fundamental constituent of existence: power. The individual who strives for a better life must understand that all external battles are but a mad cult, for any inward victory inevitably reshapes one's outward reality. Conversely, if everyone were to let external stimuli shape their inner drives, the world would become a mirror image of replication; soulless, monotonous, void of originality. In other words, so long as the world is governed by the force of the interior, it remains certain that it cannot be wholly corrupted by futility. Uselessness wanders through the absurdity of the crowds, but no personal struggle ever gives substance to the void. For this reason, a solitary fight possesses a gravity that sets it apart from cheap action. It becomes an affirmation that true power has yet to fully reveal its ultimate expression in this world.

The very concept of power endures through the simulation of grandeur. And it is precisely this illusion, this imaginative projection, that awakens in a person a craving to devour the inner confusions that poison ambition and foster an unbearable intolerance for discipline. First, the grand triumph is imagined. Then, power installs itself as an obsessive idea, an alluring force that summons one's attention toward self-mastery. It is a form of art, of craftsmanship, of cultivation.

The art of success is a vocation for solemnity. One must never be disheartened by the difficulty of becoming someone of value; hardship is merely the absence of the unnatural. The foundation of growth rests in what is natural, and anything corrupted can only haunt development like a scarecrow, not as a genuine barrier, but as a phantom of fear.

Once, the fear of poverty was the firm hand on the shoulder that startled and propelled every individual toward achievement. In those times, social pressure acted as the unseen force. Behind, a scarecrow of deprivation; ahead, human examples of success. As a result, society moved with far more dynamism and climbed sharply upward. Today, that beast has been domesticated. Poverty, once fierce and shivering, no longer strikes fear, it has been replaced by a chimera. And worse still, personal dignity has been shredded, even sacrificed. Humanity has adapted to its environment in accordance with the standards of modernity, transforming itself from a slayer of shortcomings into a hunter of illusions.

The awareness of poverty once held evolutionary value because it was grounded in truth, raw, undeniable reality that provoked a full reform of human attitude. But therein lies the problem of our times: it was too real. Tolerance for such brutal honesty came to be seen as intolerable, substituted instead with sweet-tasting delusions. Why should one endure the harshness of truth when they can be numbed by the comfort of illusion? This is where we've arrived. Even when a person lives in dismal poverty, it no longer terrifies them, they are distracted by seductive stimulants. They live not to escape lack, but to flirt with deception. Reality is easy to ignore, but greatness is unreachable for those who fail to see it clearly. To make ignorance a way of life is the highest joy of failure.

Ordinary people are often separated from success by a very simple truth: no matter how deeply they desire it, they are not repulsed by a life of lack. On the contrary, they begin to develop abnormal cravings that make scarcity seem appealing. They either obsess over trifles or dream grandly without effort, both of which distort reality. Some beam with delight over the insignificant; others long for magnificence while doing nothing to deserve it, sunk in a pitiful condition. In such climates, success never visits where there's an appetite for distortion.

A diet of superficiality nourishes a particular kind of system, one that neither starves nor strengthens but merely deceives. Yet it must be said: purging oneself of superficiality is a purification possible only for the strong. Only they can withstand the pressure of raw reality and live with the sharp ambition of full lucidity. No weak character can endure the absence of the inessential. It is strength, and strength alone, that makes man fit for any place in the world.

A superficial craving, under society's standards, manifests as a lust for luxury. There is no hunger sharper in today's world. A grand house, a powerful car, designer clothes, extravagant vacations—these thoughts stir unease in anyone who dares to compare themselves with others. At once, such fixations can be born from achievement, desperation, or downfall. Luxury is not within everyone's reach; its price is steep, and the devotion it demands arises from a radical firmness of will. While fleeing poverty may once have been a healthy reflex, sprinting toward opulence risks awakening an incurable affliction: the most corrupt form of unbeing that can exist. A monstrous incarnation of dark ambition: a creature that tramples everything underfoot, void of human values, scheming evil for personal gain.

No one, of their own accord, can or should forget the supreme forces that govern existence. Man is claimed by what he inspires, and the supernatural powers, whether benevolent or malevolent, repay him, inevitably and justly, with exactly what his existence warrants. Divine assistance is always granted, but only in return for a hard-fought struggle. Only through toil is need reshaped until the integrity of lack becomes a kind of dishonesty. He who has worked relentlessly for what he desires can only be a prosperous man of virtue. True—but this truth must be expanded. Has every successful figure in the world earned their path through labor alone? Certainly not. Therefore, there must be another route.

The world is not influenced solely by forces of good; the malevolent, too, have their own offer. And their promise is seductive: the supreme evil gives things far more easily, but at a much higher cost: the soul. And the most frequent currency in that exchange? Luxury. It's incomprehensible how some choose to devalue the very essence of life within them for a cheap abundance of things.

In folk culture, the supreme spirit of evil is imagined in stark contrast to what it peddles: a grotesque, hideous, terrifying, annihilating figure. Yet it corrupts not through horror, but through opulence, dazzling, charming, radiant, and beguiling illusions. The heat of hell is felt not through disgust, but through excess. Human beings are instinctively repulsed by ugliness, which, through an aesthetic leaning, leaves them vulnerable to deception by enchantment. For this reason, the most effective collapse of human civilization that evil could orchestrate would come through its most beautiful creation in this world: the woman.

With an army of angel-faced women, the forces of darkness orchestrate the unleashing of ultimate doom. This does not mean that the final victory will be diabolical, nor that all can be corrupted, but it marks the deepest vulnerability of the human race. If deception were a mousetrap, then beauty would be humanity's cheese. The most frequent components in the architecture of success are alluring snares. Man's perception is wholly captured by the visual spectrum. Daydreaming in darkness leads to awakening by revelation, by illumination; but dreaming with eyes closed about the shine of luxury descends into madness. History itself contemplates the monomania for gold, diamonds, opulence, and a life built on extravagance.

Luxury, in the hands of the strong, would not be something to condemn, for they possess the discipline to master both it and themselves. They acquire it through integrity, untouched by malice, and with the wisdom to keep it from corrupting their nature. But in the hands of the weak, luxury becomes society's most effective weapon for spreading decay and dread. It is fertile soil for malevolent forces to flourish, for the masses are insufficiently cultivated to harvest abundance without losing their sanity in the process. From this extravagantly costly way of life sprouts the rot of individuation, a fatal exasperation born of materialism; bringing forth the sour fruit of villainy and the hollow shell of moral insignificance.

Regardless of whether prosperity is gained through virtue or vice, it carries with it a shadow when viewed from the outside. Envy and resentment toward those who have achieved success, by any means, are widespread social parasites. They create internal discomfort, distort perception, and breed a false understanding of reality. For no one truly sees the lives of the accomplished, they only glimpse the glittering surface. Success is bark; the internal struggles are its roots. Envy would wither if people split open the core before being seduced by the sweetness of the fruit.

One sees another's success and grows bitter, but never pauses to consider that the person may be drowning in stress, suffocating under responsibility, or locked in battle with time. Another walks past an imposing house and mutters, "Some people have all the luck," unaware that behind those walls lives a man wrestling with thoughts of suicide. Somewhere else, a woman looks at her friend's seemingly perfect family and is consumed with jealousy, imagining her friend's husband to be the ideal man, never suspecting he might be unfaithful at every opportunity.

For one, the eggs have gone stale; for another, the pearls are out of fashion. Indeed, everyone bears their own burdens, trivial or tragic, light or heavy, real or imagined. What matters is not the weight of another's troubles but the tending of one's own. The steward of a village is not he who peers over the fence at another's wealth, but he who measures the gaps in his own yard.

Success has no secret, it has a principle, a singular competition: the man who labors today so that tomorrow he may surpass the man he was yesterday. Obsessing over others brings no reward; it only fattens into an unbearable burden. Character dilutes in shallowness and shrinks in fulfillment. No man awakens his intelligence while the winds of envy howl through his mind. Envy, then, is but a nickname for chosen foolishness.

The most you gain comes when you wager on yourself. Personal investment is the bankruptcy of all shortcomings. Risk, persistence, ambition, suffering, stubbornness, and vitality, these are the currencies of realization. They cannot be shared, nor can they be disputed when the victor stands triumphant. Success, in its most authentic form, is built in solitude, step by step. There are times when the influence of another may shift the natural flow of one's path to glory, but once in the arena, the favored individual sweats alone—and it is there, in solitude, that they understand: help does not come anymore. It is also alone that they realize whether they are nearing triumph.

Man can become the oracle of his own success—in that moment when he no longer recognizes himself. It happens quietly, during the slow march of growth, when he pauses in bewilderment amidst a vast emptiness, sighing. He looks around: no one. He seeks help: absence. He glances at the clock: time has passed. He inhales deeply, closes his eyes, looks inward, and is struck: *"Who is this person I've become?"* At that moment, with that question, consciousness signals a revelation, the former self is no longer, it lives only in memory, and achievement is nearer than ever. To be astonished by oneself is the foretelling of success; a notice written in the omen of becoming.

In the end, the merit of the victor can only be denied through absurdity, and the one who has lost can only condemn themselves for not having tried harder. The spring of fulfillment flows with every drop of sweat. Admiration and reverence for hardship generate waves of effort.

Yet, when it comes to action, people often fall into mass delusion, mistaking difficulty for ignorance. Were failure a result of unknowing alone, it would be venerable. What renders it blameworthy is man's rejection of knowledge; rationalized and excused like a coward hiding behind the illusion that "it's too hard." In truth, very few things in this world are genuinely hard. Most are simple, almost banal, in their essence. Anyone willing to look beyond the veil of appearance will come to this realization on their own. Difficulty is real and must be overcome, but it is widely misinterpreted. Where one man sees a challenge as impossible, countless others tackle it with ease. That reveals the truth: it isn't hard, it's just unknown.

Just as a joke loses its humor when told a second time, pain too loses its power when endured again. Nothing is earned without effort, not in this world. No achievement precedes labor, and no striving is possible without work. Every impotence stems from one: the fear of toil, the fear of the hard. But suffering should not be feared, it should be honored. It is the dignified excuse that allows one to escape the stagnant dance of incompetence. In the rhythm of human accomplishment, the steps of struggle are the beat of resounding results.

In the end, everything and nothing boils down to one thing: effort, or the lack of it. Everything else is lamentation. Whether up or down, behind or ahead, in any position, failure or success stems from a single origin: motivation.

As a practical justification, motivation emerged as an alibi for laziness. Man feels uneasy wearing the label of someone who's in conflict with work, not because of an inner dilemma, but because of the social discomfort of being pointed at. His own opinion doesn't trouble him; the gaze of others boils his insides. And, as always, words are easier than deeds. If he cannot overcome his inertia, at least let him triumph in semantics: "I'm lazy" evolved into "I lack motivation." The same horror of success, but rephrased in a hopeful tone—less condemning, more forgiving. We seek motivation and we shall succeed! To seek something sounds more alluring than to fight against something. Even better, seeking externalizes the problem, it is no longer his burden. If he says "I'm looking for something," it implies it isn't within him. Laziness, on the other hand, pins the issue to his chest like a shameful badge. And yet, the lazy man makes as much noise as a flea's sneeze.

"Motivation" is just one of many examples where language distorts reality. It was born from weakness, from a lack of fortitude in the face of truth. Human inferiority reveals itself in the artful manufacturing of excuses and illusions. Animals don't enjoy that luxury, they wouldn't survive. Imagine the state of nature if a lion told its cub, "I'll hunt, but I'm not quite motivated yet." The difference between nature and society lies in the intensity of action. In the jungle, life doesn't wait; it acts. Spontaneous, unfiltered, unapologetic. For the beast, there is no tomorrow. In society, man contemplates, hesitates, stretches plans to infinite timelines, avoids critique, and breeds pretense.

If he's not skilled enough to fabricate the illusion himself, he'll relish hearing it from others. Thus arose a modern trend disguised as a profession: the motivational speaker. A performance, nothing more. Its only value lies in theatrics, no one finds success through the voices of others. The only people who act on the words of another are those who have masters or bosses. The autonomous act only through thought. Everything falls apart or rises again in the mind. The failure and the accomplished alike have wandered their fates through the same neural pathways.

The mirror reflects to man the most inscrutable truth, the very reason his life stands in ruin. He may deceive others, but never himself. Any lie, excuse, or discouragement spoken inwardly becomes a seductive force, one that lures him gently but relentlessly into the arms of failure. Alone, before his reflection, he cannot shield himself from truth; if he does, he becomes inert, incapable of seeing anything through. The mirror can be a powerful tool, if it is used for self-criticism, not for vanity. When obsession with image replaces honest introspection, man projects nothing more than a ghost of what he could become.

Self-criticism is the wind that breathes aspiration into the psyche. Through it, thought becomes dense, chiseled, and rich with bold ideas. A sculpted mentality turns burden into mastery. Every hardship is reshaped through the sharpness of thought, and from the depths of mental agility arises the spark to illuminate vagueness. In contrast, an unworked mind crafts a landscape defined by humiliation and defeat, a bitter fate paralyzed by the fear of losing life's wonder.

Mental evolution is not optional, it is imperative. Without it, the path forward becomes dangerously stagnant. If man has a goal, a direction, an aim, then there is no greater tool than the refined mind. Every achievement that stems exclusively from persistence, clarity, and intellectual growth becomes a destination transcended, charged with meaning and set on a course diverging from regression. A refined mentality pushes one further than any plan could predict; the call to return, to retreat, fades naturally with each step forward.

Expansive thinking acts as a centrifugal force, casting us

away from the dull center of life, from that accessible zone of existence where ease meets resignation, and where many settle, content to merely exist. It is simple to remain stuck. It is arduous to move forward, step by step. That is why failure is easy, and success, exacting.

In general, through positive discrimination, society acknowledges the merits of the successful individual. Every achievement is credited to their own effort; all upright minds agree that such a person has earned their place through merit and perseverance, unless they are accused, rightly or not, of cheating. The prevalence of positive discrimination is a sign of progressive tendencies, a signal that society is distancing itself from the suspicion of fraud. However, the same measure is rarely applied in reverse. Failure is almost never regarded as a personal outcome in collective discourse, except when it ought to be. Those who have been wholly defeated by life for reasons beyond their control are rare exceptions; those who have ruined themselves are the prevailing norm. A person who never wastes a chance, no matter how small, to learn, to improve, does not end up in irrelevance. Consistent progress reveals itself over time. Every effort leads somewhere, and persistence is the surest path to a distant destination. Every action has a consequence, and no psychic or physical mobilization can merge with a vacuum. Everything a person does has an imprint on their being.

Thus, what man truly needs is a direction, a purpose toward which he advances slowly and steadily. And by doing so, he guarantees his distance from failure. Because failure is not just an outcome, but the denial of the journey itself, the easiest excuse to evade the discomfort of confronting one's own identity. Realization, on the other hand, is the path paved with risks, the bold pursuit of a new self. It is the hardest undertaking: to move forward through uncharted conditions, constantly reassessing the next step along the way. The journey is not necessarily pleasant, nor easy, nor free of obstacles. Paradise is never found in "nowhere," but in "beyond"—in the precise direction one dares to aim.

Man is a servant on the road and a master at its end. But often, he takes ten steps forward only to be pushed twenty back. Advancement is like a torn sack that leaks what it gathers along the journey; in which case, there is only one solution to arrive with it still full, he must pour in more than he loses. This sliding into regression continues until he becomes immovable before the current obstacle. The further he aims to go, the larger the sack grows, and so does the hole. Those who carry nothing in their pack are those who have avoided action or waited endlessly for opportunity, and they have no one to blame but themselves.

The world defines itself as an immense complexity of events that cannot result without a singular trigger: action. No effect comes without a cause. The link between action and outcome has been demonstrated and consecrated in Newton's Third Law—a fundamental law of the universe. This law states that when one body exerts a force on another, the second body exerts an equal and opposite force back upon the first. In other words, whatever effort is made upon something, that something will respond, and return the gesture to its source. When one engages in physical activity, the consequences appear on the body itself; the same applies to intellectual pursuits, which mold the mind into distinction. The greater the force of action, the more grand the result.

With that said, in a more accurate phrasing, the failed man

is not guilty of not seeking success, he is guilty of not applying effort. No one can be defeated by failure if they continue to expend energy toward a purpose. It would defy nature itself for a person to remain irrelevant in a competitive world that ascends in greatness through individual struggle. Without work, man exists in the homeland of nothingness; with work, he becomes an exile in achievement.

Success is built with patience and waiting; time is not an enemy, but rather a chosen ally to be embraced. All grandeur and infinite personal fulfillment are filled drop by drop through the passing of time, nothing majestic pours or floods in the process of accumulation, and duration renders the imminent attainable. Any success on the verge of materializing carries one undeniable truth: elapsed time. The issue for many lies not only in misunderstanding their resources, but in being misled by their environment. You don't grasp the value of a drop in the jungle, but in the desert, you worship it. Success must be inflated where obtainable things carry meaning.

Nature shows no mercy to those who give up easily; it punishes them harshly. In a dire survival scenario, anyone lives and breathes with a constant gun to their head named "giving up", and the one who pulls the trigger is none other than themselves. The moment the thought of surrender begins to circulate through their mind, it marks the start of a countdown, until everything stops, until their journey in this world ends.

In a similar situation, though absent the risk of literal death, lies the one seeking fulfillment. Except here, the gun isn't to the head, it's aimed at the feet. No one reaches any destination when they shoot their own ability to move forward. Two things alone can stop a person from taking another step: death and giving up.

As long as one lives, they cannot merge with the idea of losing hope, which, in essence, is nothing more than the remedy that renders one immune to discouragement. As old age creeps in, man slowly lets go of boldness and instead clings to appeasement. Resignation doesn't arise from biology or aging, but from the absence of the ambition to surpass oneself. At any age, one can reach an unexpected apex, provided they are not satisfied, not at peace with what they are, and still desire more. If success were tied to time remaining, it would be reserved only for the young—which reality clearly disproves.

Experience and time are existential currencies to be used in favor of the disheartened, upheld as the highest admiration for the supreme joy of daring. What does one have to lose by investing trust, mind, and time into an attempt? No more than a bee changing orchards.

Even more so, the brain defies the rigidity of physical laws, it transcends them. It is a phenomenon that knows no limits, capable of creating what can hardly be explained. Problems once thought eternal are solved by a spark of insight. The mind can make time relative and render experience obsolete; what one learns in a week, another can grasp in a day; what one fails to accomplish in a lifetime, another achieves in a month. A single brief thought can trigger an overwhelming cascade of actions. No one can truly predict what life may offer, each has their destiny, and some are gifted with unforeseen peaks at unexpected stages.

Therefore, man must have patience, must wait, must keep hope alive, and treat time not with blame, but with understanding, for nothing is ever certain in life, and success can emerge anywhere, anytime. Unforeseen.

There are only two things man longs to postpone indefinitely: the beginning and the death. He sees only the stretch between birth and death as an attraction, a privilege, excluding both ends. He can delay the start until the end, but he cannot postpone death forever. Procrastination grants man only the regard of the yet-to-arrive. Everything else, the delay, the indecision, turns his life into a monologue preempting a fate defeated by hesitation. In the battle for triumph, success, or achievement, procrastination is the mother of all wars; undeniably ending the fight if lost. This is why every person should become aware of the countless collateral damages caused by each day of delay. And then, with sweat and pain, combat every second, minute, hour, day, or night, not to surrender to the uncertain "someday," but to be overtaken by the urgent "now."

As such, life is a struggle, and no one escapes suffering. Either you suffer for what you want, straining for a favorable result, or you suffer in hardship, living a life of nothingness. Each person chooses their pain, one of the few things in life truly within your control. And always remember, as a spark of illumination: success only shines if, when you were in the dark, you lit your path with a smile.

7

Wealth

We live in an age where the planet spins in rhythm with money. Life experiences are now commodities, and any thesis on human existence in the modern era that omits the importance of money becomes void of meaning, sense, or purpose. Material wealth distorts perceptions of happiness, love, and freedom—and this distortion seduces anyone with a hunger for "more" into a relentless chase for possession. Money is a tangible paradox: with it, the harshness of reality is forgotten, while experiential knowledge is etched into memory.

It's impossible to say with certainty whether the arrival of money in someone's life brings good or ill, it may be either, or both. Yet the 21st-century citizen is socially compelled into a race to earn a living. The pursuit of money needed for daily survival comes with a steep cost: hardship, fatigue, stress, health, and often, the sacrifice of time. This marathon has no clear finish line.

A common linguistic fable claims that "everything has a price in money." If that were true, then is nothingness priceless? If so—how terrifying, how sublime. Things do not have a price; they have a numeric reference value. Money has a price, and it is paid not just in currency but in time, effort, sacrifice, and strain. Sacrifice being the most critical of all.

Moreover, there is no universal standard in the world of money. All its attributes are locked in relativity. The material realm refuses allegiance with pragmatism; it thrives in ambiguity. This often gives rise to perceptions that diverge from objective reality, not necessarily falsehoods, but flights into fiction. And fiction, by nature, does not align fully with fact. It is a means of importing reality and consciously reshaping it into stylized expressions of truth.

A person fractures their own reality when they let money steer their life. Their imagination begins to derail when their mind is entirely oriented toward wealth. And since no one can integrate into society without a means of compensation, income becomes a tool that enriches imagination but weakens clarity—a volatile lens through which life is perceived. In this sense, we may all be destined to live cornered by circumstance, under the shadow of thoughts designed more for acceptance, consolation, or conviction that existence itself conforms to a subjective valuation.

On the scale of perception used to assess the importance of things, money stands firmly at the top. There is nothing with greater impact, power, or influence in classifying nearly everything than the monetary unit. The numerical value assigned to a product shapes both the understanding and the desire one develops toward it. A garment is seen one way when its price is unknown, and quite another when the cost is revealed. An expensive car draws more interest, just as a painting appraised at a high sum becomes the centerpiece of attention. An artistic creation may be sold on a street corner or dazzle in a museum; meaning, ultimately, that the cost of a work of art also ranks its creator within the pyramid of success.

Give a modest person an ordinary, inexpensive watch and he'll wear it effortlessly. Give him a luxury watch with a staggering price tag, and he'll wear it with anxiety—his hand will tremble, cold sweats may follow, and his behavior will become uneasy, stressed by the fear of losing or having it stolen.

Ordinary people don't know how to behave when placed, even briefly, into a life that stretches far beyond the horizon of their familiar experience. As such, the sudden appearance of wealth produces a kind of psychological shock, followed by erratic behavior. Just because something is difficult to obtain, because it requires a large sum, doesn't necessarily mean it's valuable. But undeniably, the range of behaviors exhibited by the one who owns it expands, either in confidence or in absurdity. Life begins to adopt new meanings, distorted under the influence of money.

A cheap coat and a coat that's several times more expensive may serve the same functional purpose, but they will not matter equally to the same person. The psychological phenomenon of sensory awareness in evaluating the world becomes shaped by assigning importance based on financial classification. In other words, humans rely on the monetary lens to reshape their reality and live through illusion. The truth remains: an expensive coat warms just as well as a cheap one. But a single label can forge an unequal, irreparable, and unstable perception.

Society might have remained clear-sighted if money disturbed only lifeless things, if its reach had ended with the tangible. But the descent from vitality into a dehumanized state begins when money touches the soul. A moment of sorrow, satisfaction, gratitude, appreciation, or disdain toward an object is part of the ordinary inner motion of the mind. Yet the true abyss, the one that opens into a realm both inhuman and uncertain, gapes wide when the human soul is consumed by the craving for wealth.

When money distorts joy or love, the spirit becomes barren. The hinges that hold the gate between our world and hell are the feelings welded within the house of money. Greed, envy, malice, hatred, and egotism find their way into the soul when that gate is opened by a mind locked to reason. Such negative emotions wouldn't spread like a contagion if people were strong, diligent, and capable. But when corruption pierces the organic structure of a human being, what is revealed is the horrifying reality of possession—not of wealth, but by it.

Only a soul already conquered by darkness can survive such inner tension. Indeed, man is the only being in existence capable of embodying a density of evil bigger than that in hell itself. And the smallest vessel able to hold that darkness is the human heart. In that light, a weakened, venal world may be more densely packed with malevolence than the eternal inferno.

Therefore, it may be said that a character stripped of strength is a greater threat than money itself—for money, after all, is merely a tool. The axe holds no concern for what trees it cuts.

Even human relationships cannot escape this hazard. The danger grows real when wealth begins to fracture bonds formed by birth or alliance. Brotherhood, friendship, and marriage may all blur when the warmth of money cools the soul and casts a frost over intimacy. Love and joy can wither in financial climates; some may even freeze entirely.

Many parents have denied their second child a life simply to preserve the inheritance for one. Many impassioned romances never began because one heart was dismissed for its modest means. Countless friendships were never born, their seeds stifled by disparity in fortune.

The fact that certain relationships never formed holds no weight, no emotional charge, there's nothing to mourn in a bond that lived only in the imagination. These could-have-beens are phantom threads in the fabric of possibility, and thus leave behind no pain. Far removed from such sentimental irrelevance, however, are the bonds once real, once close, now shattered by wealth. Here, suffering ascends to dreadful peaks: when brothers fall out and go silent, when spouses part ways and give birth to hatred, when friends turn into enemies. Most often, such repulsion arises when thoughts begin to ride in tandem with money.

Wealth and poverty alike bypass the essence of being human. And when no inner defender stands watch, both carve their names into the register of social status. Every interaction in society is first filtered through material condition, rarely through human value. No one can deny that we adjust our behavior depending on another's financial standing. But this tendency is not merely social, it is deeply personal. After all, people behave differently toward themselves when their own fortunes shift. Why, then, would they treat others any differently?

Everyone carries a mindset, a voice, a manner shaped by

their economic circumstances. As one climbs the social ladder, subtle evolutions of thought occur. Financial status shapes the human psyche with remarkable power, wealth can cast long shadows over virtue, and brighten the blemishes of one's character. Cheerfulness, kindness, humility, and sincerity are more often found among the downtrodden and grow increasingly rare among the affluent.

Some are good because they are poor; others turn cruel because they are rich—such is the seduction of corruption. There is no guarantee that a person praised for their humble character in poverty will retain the same spirit in wealth. Money reveals human essence; it brings to light the true quality of a person with rumination, far less by separation. Judged objectively and critically, it offers one of the most reliable lenses through which to foresee the substance of a person.

The most foolish are those who are cruel in poverty, they're easily recognized by their envy, for they have nothing behind them, no foundation of power. The most dangerous, however, are those who carry cruelty into wealth, they wield power as a weapon. And the pinnacle of humanity? It lies in those who, despite possessing great fortune, remain kind, humble, and grounded. For when immense power meets enduring goodness, one encounters a person of true worth.

Money is a factory of problems and the product that resolves them. It holds, simultaneously, the power to sow malignant influence in the lives of some and undeniable benefit in the lives of others. Everything depends on the hands that harvest it. There is no seed more fertile in raising the quality of life than currency itself. Freedom, comfort, experience, mental development, and the overall refinement of living can be profoundly elevated through wealth.

Therefore, if the same fructification can grow to two opposing effects, poisoning in one case, vitaminization in another, it means that toxicity lies not in the fruit itself, but in the cultivation technique. The saying "Money is the root of all evil" is most often uttered by those who fixate on the fruit, not the soil. The foundation of corruption is not money, it is human weakness. Humanity would still perpetrate wrongdoings even in the absence of wealth. The mind is more vividly marked by demonic deeds than by benevolent ones, which is why so many assume that riches must inevitably carry wickedness rather than goodness.

Yet history is not as lopsided as it may appear. Malevolent acts may simply cling more tightly to memory. Devote your life to good and commit one misdeed, and it will be the latter that etches your name in time. A king may have averted a hundred wars and launched only one, yet history remembers him for that single conflict. Both war and culture require funding, one brings horror to the world, the other beauty and harmony.

If a supreme force ever sought to destroy humanity, the simplest method would be this: reshape society so that weakness becomes the norm. Through the frail, evil would spread; through the strong, a better age could be received. Civilization can only thrive on an economic foundation—yet that same base, left to rot, can cause collapse. Great things can be built when intentions are pure and people are strong enough to resist corruption. Thus, society must cultivate citizens of integrity, capable, resilient, and morally grounded, so that malevolence finds no fertile ground. Only when this condition is met does the beneficent power of money shine brighter than its shadow.

If animals used money, fish would either drown or fly. Currency is a tool that can shatter the limits of life, or pierce the threshold of death. Like any instrument, it demands training; without it, even the noblest object becomes an agent of harm in unskilled hands. No one arrives in this world already masterful. Everything must be learned—starting with the most basic: how to walk on one's own feet. To seek wealth before shaping one's character reveals nothing more than a disordered ambition. The individual must first journey inward, before pursuing the outward. When an undeveloped personality immerses itself in the illusion of wealth, it becomes entangled in deception, driven toward collapse, plagued by obsessive thought, agitated by inner confusion, and deprived of clarity.

A person can reach extraordinary destinations in life when their financial path runs parallel with inner evolution. Equilibrium is sustained only when certain virtues are present: discipline, self-command, calmness, lucidity, and prudence. In their absence, money becomes the roulette wheel of fate—spinning lives into chaos, placing control not in the individual, but in the hands of randomness. In the hands of the swayer, wealth becomes a tremendous force; a building block of personal built fate. With it, one may turn every wall into a foundation for new construction. Bend toward yourself, and you will stand upright before fate. Bow to possessions, and you will carry destiny like a burden.

The error of many lies in the way they chase money. Just as paper scattered on the ground is blown away when someone runs toward it, wealth, too, obeys the laws of physics—it flees the frantic. Life must be interpreted through the logic of gravity: if one desires something, they must increase their weight, deepen their worth, and that which they seek will be drawn toward them. This is the Universe's own law: things are pulled by density, not by lightness. Love, happiness, and wealth flow toward those with spiritual gravity. Fortune is attracted, not attacked. A wise person in the financial realm learns to balance the two polarities of every banknote, spending and investing, and thereby transforms into a magnet for money. Those who understand money beyond mere need are often liberated internally, yet sentenced externally to a life within abundance's gilded cage.

All things sprout in the mind, and thinking is the irrigation. Every opportunity to reflect is a drop that nourishes consciousness, preventing the mind from drying out. A popular saying observes: "You're poor even in thought." The wealthy often spend more time in analysis, reading, debate, and inquiry, habits that stimulate the soul, while the impoverished may be drawn to distractions, trivial indulgences, or addiction. Even when the wealthy rightly credit themselves, others rarely acknowledge those merits genuinely—only superficially. Perhaps this is natural, since true understanding is rarely present. Beneath visible success lie layered ambitions, weighty and hidden. Those who delve deeply into the roots of success are the ones who ultimately secure a life enriched with enduring material well-being.

Money is a source of existence that depletes hope while enriching experience. What remains for the wealthy to hope for? And what experiences can the poor accumulate? In life, the one who masters the art of finance becomes an active classic, etched into the present with visible effect, while the one trained in lack becomes an unceasing wanderer, unemployed by life's offerings. The rich often live outwardly, immersed in the external realm, while the poor survive with what they find within: hopes, desires, dreams—everything that elevates their spirit just enough to obscure the cruelty of reality.

The fear of having an infinite opportunity to live without meaning becomes, paradoxically, a liberation from the tyranny of deceptive allurements. For the impoverished, the first spark of initiative is often the awareness of time and the haunting realization that it's being denied through the absence of lived experience.

The human being cannot comprehend eternity. The infinite lies beyond reason's grasp, and only religion offers a narrative for it, because man is small in an absolute Universe. His life reduces to constructing a limited comfort bubble, far from the despair that comes from wrestling with the unknowable.

To step outside this bubble is, for the rich, to puncture it, and there is often only one consequence: a return to poverty. The world is fluid, volatile, and fiercely competitive. Wealth is not boundless. It circulates in finite quantities, distributed in ever-shifting fragments across economic structures. If one increases their financial power, somewhere else, another, or several others, experience depletion. A society composed entirely of the poor or entirely of the rich, without economic polarity, is a utopia; impossible to realize.

This reality is reflected in the 80/20 rule, which states that 80% of a nation's wealth is held by 20% of its population. An unwritten law. A chaotic order. A brilliant principle forged to protect the world from slipping into the abyss of absolute disorder. Thus, the conclusion can be shaped into a simple notion: not all can become rich, just as not all are doomed to poverty. Coexisting with the idea of remaining destitute is only possible through endurance. Living in abundance, meanwhile, demands a nearly unbearable responsibility. Both states are fragile and susceptible to collapse. The first, through dismay and desperation. The second, through ungoverned excess and the loss of moderation.

For someone familiar with poverty, money is like a stranger—unfamiliar until directly encountered. At first, when a person meets a stranger, they may carry a hopeful, positive outlook; but as the layers of interaction unfold, that view inevitably gathers shadows of doubt. Naturally, no one can predict the extent of someone's malice until it reveals itself. In other words, ignorance is a cloak of protection that aids in the exploitation of naivety. It's not flawed to believe a stranger might be good, what's flawed is assuming they cannot be harmful. Evil must be kept in plain sight so the eyes may stay fixed upon it; every move tracked, every shift anticipated. Evil left unattended becomes a knife at your back—silent, sudden, and devastating.

Material wealth means the constant nearness of money, and if not kept in view, it blinds the conscience. It distorts one's moral compass, leading to a life overburdened by the exaggerated reverence for unstable paper. The wealthy often lose sight of humanity, of core values, staring instead into the shimmering fog of uncertainty, into surfaces that shift from good to dangerous without warning. This makes them, potentially, uncontrollably adrift. A hidden sliver of naivety is enough to crown absurd dependence in the kingdom of the blind.

A good financial state does not come with the guarantee of an improved life, it can worsen it if clarity of vision and thought is absent. A life governed in darkness is doomed to get lost in it. Everyone should learn how to sense money, feel it, know it, understand it, before wielding its power. Otherwise, they become complicit in their own disillusionment. Innocence is devoid of the wealthy, just as no poor soul has ever stepped into primacy.

Thus, money introduces confusion into the perception of those who've never handled it. Expectations may be high; the impact, low—or vice versa. In rare cases, the most cautious fear that wealth brings only burden, not blessing.

Wealth reveals itself through every human sense. The easiest recognition comes through sight: the affluent wear an appearance that reflects the height of their wallet. Then comes sound—money sings in a silent orchestra. Its presence fills a space not with noise, but with an austere quiet. Where great fortunes reside, silence often dominates. Clamor is native to places of misery; wealth favors stillness.

Like hearing, smell too can detect the economic state of a place. Extreme poverty carries a literal stench, an absence of means made pungent. Luxury, by contrast, imposes itself through fragrances—delicate, curated, refined. Even taste becomes a barometer: the quantity, quality, and sophistication of a meal betray its cost. An abundant table is a symphony of refined indulgence.

And finally, wealth is perhaps most vividly felt through touch, through the comfort it grants, the softness it affords, the textures of ease and abundance. Money, though silent, speaks through everything the body can sense.

Money digs into happiness, sows liberty, and buries worry. The quality of life is profoundly shaped by financial awareness, for wealth transforms existence into an upward curve, a refined rhythm of ease, security, and control. As abundance grows, the human perspective shifts; the one who thrives in surplus struggles to understand how others survive with less. Scarcity becomes an alien notion. The refusal to accept restraint morphs into a subtle seduction of the self, an unceasing pursuit of material expansion.

The saying "money doesn't bring happiness" seems often whispered by those who have never had it, or perhaps invented by them. For the wealthy, fortune is a marriage to comfort, and if happiness enters the picture at all, she is more likely a mistress than a wife. Still, this phrase was never meant to uplift the soul above materialism, but rather to discourage the drive toward economic competition. With or without wealth, life must be lived. No one has the right to tether joy to their finances. To mourn over money is to suffer the price of comparison. Without it, financial status would be a simple point of reference, not a chasm of discontent stretching endlessly between people.

Yes, there are things—real, meaningful things—that may bring greater fulfillment than money. But the lack of money creates a condition of such severity that its absence cannot be ignored. Even if one believes wealth won't guarantee happiness, its pursuit is still wise—for it delivers a myriad of gifts that soften reality with a tranquil smile. Money doesn't buy happiness, but it does sell off most sources of unhappiness.

A full wallet expands one's social freedom and dissolves empirical limitations. It extinguishes the fear of tomorrow, alleviates the weight of debt, and frees the mind from the tyranny of budgeting every coin. Financial strength strikes boldly at the heart of one's ability to own their time. It offers command over how to spend the day, how to waste the night, or how to reverse both.

When life is shackled to a paycheck, shaped by the rhythm of wages and routines, personal freedom becomes conditional. One's capacity to live spontaneously, to choose time rather than be ruled by it, is vastly diminished. Money, then, is not merely a tool of trade, it is a sculptor of autonomy, a silent arbiter of how a life is built or bound.

At the base of the pyramid of the benefits brought by money lies autonomy. The wealthy man surrounds himself with countless advantages, but nothing honors the human vocation more than independence—to not depend on the company of fellow men who, in many cases, are clothed in the thinking of jesters. All those who experience the profound feeling of not being bound to anyone, in the sense of subjugation, live life in miraculous uniqueness. In a time when society has become a mechanism stripped of originality, where people's role is to serve as a lubricant to maintain the functioning of the economic engine, the fate of the one who self-directs represents an extraordinary phenomenon of piloting one's own thoughts and actions.

The one caught in a breakdown of allowance lives without the power of personal decisions, whether radical or minor, his time managed by pre-established social constructs, and the only control he holds is limited to choosing among what others offer him.

A life lived in dependency, whatever it may be, is one sunk in comfort because thought and action are estranged from drive, and the one who lives and earns his existence by doing only what others say, fueled by a sufficient dose of personal need satisfaction, develops an attitude of inertia.

A human condition refers to reason, and how can someone be rational if they are deprived of independence in thought?

Only a fool considers the most important use of money to be tied to material status, to luxury, to comfort, to the abundance of things and boundless consumption. A watch, a car, or a garment can be expensive and at the same time void of value; anyone will eventually grow bored of any car, no matter how costly. Living in a grand house and in a zone atypical to the common isn't trivial, nor is it a detachment from the meaning of wealth, but in the end, all people who spend life in a select area reach habituation; the sensation of grandeur contracts. In contrast, far from the tangible, in the center of the infinite abstract, is independence, which disputes with no one and listens solely to human necessity. The man who quarreled with freedom has sat in counsel with foolhardiness.

Dependence on society can be measured by the degree of integration an individual simulates. All people fake some part of themselves to enter social groups, circles of friends, workplaces, or other communities. Is there a person who isn't pretending when seeking to be included in a group? Really? Who—perhaps the drunkard?

Society is a paradox, a fortunate one, in which people recognize each other without knowledge. No one truly knows the one they call close, that individual shaped by repeated interactions. Closeness is a benefit of imperceptible pretense. All people hide inhuman inner realities, and if fellow humans had a "divine eye" to see them, relationships would become a noose for unraveling.

What value would human connections still hold if they began

from the contemplation of ideals, rather than being grounded in the deepest of authentic convictions? Pretense has saved man from isolation in the abyss of disassociation. It's not ideal, moral, or admirable, but it's a mystical manipulation, comparable to childhood's unconsciousness. You have no reason to be disturbed that you don't truly know your friends; rather, you should be entirely at peace that you don't. If the bonds were based on truth, you wouldn't need them. Their fakeness is the reason you have friends.

Just like in childhood, learning, evolution, maturation, and character development are reactions to the lessons and revelations arising from temporary obscurity. In adulthood, close relationships serve as guarantees that one won't be left without the occasional rude awakening. A "friendly" lesson is sacred in its moment—it painfully purifies naivety.

Friends are like worries: money makes them vanish, but they return the moment you owe. No one is immune to the abandonment of friendship when venturing into the triangle of resentment, whose three vertices are: success, wealth, and truth. Friendship does not thrive through carefully verified observations but by avoiding every opportunity to say aloud what others don't want to hear, usually, the harsh truth. A person cannot hold a grudge against something true, for that would place them in parallel with accuracy and boil their conscience. Thus, the only path left for inner peace is to drive away those who spark fires with truths that hit too close to reality.

In another corner stands success, which catapults beyond any comfort once offered by friendship. A friend's peace is disturbed by the noise of another's achievement, for one who stands still cannot bear the shrill sound of a single step made through progress. And when he cannot follow the path, he changes direction, left, right, or turns his back altogether.

In the end, the third vertex, wealth, most profoundly distorts the structure of friendship. A person remembers more quickly the friend who can offer a loan and just as easily forgets the one to whom he owes a debt. He grants the most prominent seat at the table to the wealthy and isolates the one in need. The social rank of friends becomes clear in how they are treated by others in the group: the influential one is heard and placed at the center, while the modest one serves merely as filler.

Friendship—the great tragedy of money's bias. When wealth arrives in waves, truth retreats and falsehood surges in. Friendship without sincerity is like a shell stranded on the shore; eventually it decays and turns to stone.

Friendships operate through benefit, through mutual interest, not through charm alone. This means that any crack in the utility shared will shake the very foundations of emotional connection. A friend shaken by separation, especially one caused by money, often ascends the ladder to become the greatest enemy. No one harbors ill will quite like a former friend. When a man achieves something or brings a goal to completion, he must be aware: no one will despise his success more than a familiar face. Strangers are indifferent to the fate of those unknown to them.

That is why it is wise to keep one's labor and ambition quiet among friends. Otherwise, one risks being weighed down by discouragement, demoralization, and ultimately, surrender. Not everyone is well-intentioned, even if they bear the title of "friend." Some, out of obsessive envy, may oppose their companions just to keep them away from triumph. But when kept at a distance from personal ambition, acquaintances lose their power to influence the outcome. The only tool they have left is resentment.

When wealth appears suddenly, unannounced, those close to you will either envy you or rejoice for you. It's a reliable way to discern who your true friends really are.

Even so, there is no abundant life that bypasses the dynamics of human connection, or, far more rarely, the exasperating path of achieving success in utter solitude. The key that unlocks access to wealth is an idea—the mindset of forming connections so that others may open doors for you. It is the simplest and most accessible method by which a person travels through different chambers of life, gathering experience shaped by the valid realities of progress.

New people bring new openings. To keep turning in the same circle of acquaintances is to lock yourself in. There are only two ways to unfold your world into meaningful advancement: either through alignment with new people or through the grueling struggle of walking alone.

Neither cooperation nor solitude fully grasp the role of hallucinatory experiences. These states do not disturb man so deeply as to move him into action from some contradicting justification born of principle, or from the rigid order of a normatively determined world. Only through a moment of revelation does he begin to see the snare for what it is. Since reality itself is captivating through its own unrealism, it follows that absolute liberation emerges only after a struggle that shatters the spell of its enchantments. The allure of hallucination persists in a paradisiacal state just long enough that the gates of that paradise become too narrow for a mind that thinks small. And so man is left with a final, supreme condition for escape: a mad exaltation of ambition. Liberation needs no justification, it is a condition so effectively motivating, so viscerally stimulating, that any rationale becomes redundant.

Thus, a man caught in illusion has the chance to ignite a drive so powerful that it compels him to rupture the veil of delusion, to cease being the conquered and instead become the conqueror—and then, to seek wealth as a natural extension of his personal growth. Training with an invisible enemy is the ideal of a vigorous life, and the most observable foe is the hallucinatory charm of society.

Once a person has cultivated enough qualities, a diverse inner dynamism, he arrives at a position of dominion over his own existence, one that is intertwined with the operations of his mind. Illusions, hallucinations, visions, they can all serve a purpose, if one holds the awareness of their inauthenticity. They can even aid personal development. After all, without hallucinations, what would one struggle against in the beginning? Reality? Perhaps—but it strikes hard and true.

And so, if seeking the key to success through human networks is simpler, more common, more accessible, then the solitary soul must instead break the lock that binds him to the mesmerizing trance of society. This is no easy task, neither ordinary nor convenient, but one thing is certain: the most dazzling moments are those when a vision of prosperity flashes across the horizon of the ambitious. Wealth obtained through ambition owes but one debt: to consciousness.

In the end, no better method has ever been demonstrated for unlocking the secrets of experience, of existence, than lucidity itself. Delirium may nurture belief, courage, and any number of emotion-driven convictions, but a lucid mind hosts multitudes of thoughts and endures the proof. It is this endurance that makes it capable of fully transforming action. To question, to examine, to critically test all that is commonly found in society, this remains one of the most dependable paths to uncovering opportunity.

Ultimately, the rational truth is this: wealth begins in delirium, develops through lucidity, is sustained by consciousness, and ends in recklessness.

Moreover, as a conclusion confirmed time and again by intelligent judgment and inexhaustible evidence: only those who do not share in misfortune can become truly wealthy; especially those who avoid associating with the unlucky and the afflicted. Just as a life of abundance is tied to the phenomenon of connection with the extraordinary, so too is a life marked by absence and lack rooted in alliance with the ordinary masses. The only way to avoid experiencing poverty as a form of normalcy is to distance oneself from those who normalize it. In that undifferentiated zone of stagnation, no one forgives the ambition of the determined, and the beautiful states of progress are met with resentment, discouragement, and suppression—a reality that excuses the despair of a mindset where being and non-being are indistinguishable within a life dulled and demeaned.

All those who pay a high price for their experiences carry intangible debts. Paradoxical, yes—but for a simple reason: regardless of the nature of an experience, whether good or bad, the most vivid form of wealth is to be indebted to others for what they awaken in you: lessons, joy, love, revelations, even suffering. All that intensifies one's existence adds to one's true riches. The foolish notion, born of human short-sightedness, that ugly deeds must be repaid with bitterness or revenge is nothing more than a murder of potential. Once vengeance takes hold, no one listens to the meaning behind the act; no one hears the hidden message within the teaching. Why brake the chance to learn just to accelerate the hatred? What claim do you have to quantity when all your responses are petty remarks?

The truly rich man is the wise one, he who values all that others bring into his life and continues forward, unfazed by the threats of the incompetent. To be indebted to another for what they provoke within you is, in essence, a fortune of its own: a blessed fate woven with vital abundance, layered over what could have been fatal nothingness.

In another order of thoughts, some people spend what they do not have, sometimes uncontrollably. Debt is the belt that holds a man's pants up, offering the illusion of security, the reassurance that he won't be left utterly exposed. The most expensive thing an ordinary person might pay for is a house, followed by a car, and so on... yet need often collides with ability. A small income restrains great desire, and thus the only solution becomes a bargain: to sell the future in exchange for a fleeting acquisition.

Debt seduces a person toward an accessible goal; a proposition hard to refuse for the one who, in restless impatience, is obsessed with ownership. Borrowing isn't inherently wrong, nor inherently good, provided that need does not get eclipsed by want. Wanting more than necessary is often a reaction to personal irresponsibility. The future is uncertain, and the money borrowed from tomorrow may drastically increase in cost, unlike the money earned yesterday, which has already been paid in full.

Debt can act like a vitamin, a stimulant in financial metabolism, enabling growth and economic development. In such cases, it serves as a shortcut, a boost in the race of societal progress. But it can just as easily manifest as the symptom of a crisis.

The uncertainty of debt detaches money from the present moment, placing it in opposition to its intended purpose; usefulness in the now. Yet even here, perspective varies. It depends on the individual and the fruit their life bears. One truth remains indisputable: improvement comes most reliably when income increases. In that direction, the study of money becomes financial education, a safeguard against squandering the path to the future.

The presence of money wounds the journey. People, by and large, are fixated on the destination, far less on the road itself, and the sharpest, the most effective tool one might use to cut through the path, is the financial weapon. The temptation of shortcuts sneaks into the traveler's mind, a kind of impatience born from a shallow mentality that associates investment in experience with wasted time. Detouring is the coward's virtue.

Indeed, money can shorten the time it takes to obtain things, it can save hours, days, even months, but by the same token, it can impair the development of character. The children of the wealthy will benefit from abundant support, smoother roads, fewer obstacles, and a host of conveniences. But they will also inherit many behavioral gaps. Raised in selective environments, with limited exposure to the lower strata of society, their problems are swiftly resolved, and they are rarely forced to innovate in the absence of financial solutions.

At the same time, worthy of attention, almost with a violent surge, with relentless energy, hungry, seduced, fixated, pulled subjectively out of softness, is the one for whom money speaks, the one whose hunger for wealth becomes his mode of transcendence through each passing day. And in truth, what deserves praise is not the greed for money itself, but the fervor invested in making each day count. The man possessed by wealth lives each hour with overflowing intensity, driven by an inner void, by a hunger of necessity. Not so the one already sated; for he grows incapable of the tragic urgency of killing the days with purpose. Instead, he drifts, watching them expire one by one, absent any barbaric heroism. Money speaks, but the truth it tells frequently is this: ease—the peace of living by choice, not by need.

If not for the nourishment of egoism, man would not suffer so greatly under the burden of hunger for wealth. He is either a greedy egoist or a lazy one. In truth, regardless of the intensity of one's ambition to progress, especially materially, an individual demonstrates a greater concern for personal interest and often disregards the interests of others when pursuing financial satisfaction.

Paradoxically, the one who does not chase after money is often the more egoistic. The reason is simple: his admiration for simplicity, motivated by an immense pride and sustained by minimal expectations of contentment, turns his lack of desire for wealth into a fully self-centered condition—a kind of self-irony disguised as detachment. This makes the egoism of the materially indifferent more genuine: he sees only himself and contributes little, if at all, to society, directly or indirectly. Meanwhile, the egoism of the wealth-seeker is visible and apparent, yet less often acknowledged is the indirect contribution he brings to others through his material pursuits.

Egoism is an illusory state in which life caresses the curves of self-centered impulses—impulses that are often little more than symbols of naivety, lacking substance. In truth, the material struggle is more constitutive of community than of the individual. Man is transient, and boredom comes quickly. He speaks to life with moments and listens to eternity only when it quotes his name.

Perhaps during his reign, a King was criticized for his ego, his pride, or the grandeur of the castle he ordered to be built. But with time and thoughtful reflection, long after his passing, the narrative shifts, a stylistic shift into reverence. He may have lived only a few years within those walls, but the legacy remained for the nation and for generations who would pass through and admire what he left behind. So it is with everyone, even the common man. The egoism tied to wealth may seem like a fleeting fault, yet when revisited by time, it often transforms into praise.

When it comes to money, society obsessively counts personal gain and scornfully overlooks contribution. Money is not tethered to a soul, it is a social dialect. Every personal gain is a small collective benefit, just as every personal loss is a large disappointment.

It would be absurd to expect everyone to deliver full realization of their inner enthusiasm, to translate their internal fire outward, or to give more than they are willing. But just as absurd, perhaps more profoundly nonsensical, is to believe that no one is ever renegade by their own overflowing indifference.

In the end, money is little more than an occasion to satisfy our empirical ego—and a fleeting opportunity to leave a mark upon this world.

8

Faith

Within every domain lies a hidden question. In religion, it is "who?" In philosophy, "why?" In science, "how?" In medicine, "when?" In love, "how much?" In infinity, "where?" In the unknown, "what?"—and yet all may share the same answer: God. Amid the uncertainty of solving everything, in the absence of a universal truth, while preoccupied with the meaning and origin of life, sometimes even tempted by the illusion of eternity, and not least, in accepting death as a debt exchanged for the gift of having lived, humanity has dared to forge a relationship with the divine. That was the apex of human wisdom, the only idea grand enough to offer salvation: aid through the principle of persuasion.

As mankind followed the course of centuries, the concept of a Creator became subjective, relative, shaped by conditions and cultures. Religions multiplied; they became rooted in tradition, bound to peoples and lands, geographically defined. None possesses absolute truth, they seek it. Some declare that their religion is the correct path, a dialectic both inconceivable and dismissive toward others born into different directions.

Society, with all its virtues and faults, is a byproduct of a creed, for the religious influence of each individual has shaped ethics, morality, laws, conduct, and behaviors that have become woven into the fabric of social life. From the first known civilization to the present one, the stories all held a shared truth: they all believed in something. And that "something" was both spark and extinguishment. Faith in the divine molded life and made death bearable. Thus, humanity sought to erase the irrelevance from the meaning of its existence, and the only eternal compromise it ever accepted, both sufficient and limitless, was to believe in a Creator, to welcome truth clarified by belief. Without faith, truth becomes an ambition fraught with uncertainty.

Can His existence be denied? This isn't a question of *possibility*, the man can deny anything, but that does not make him right. In truth, the existence of a Creator may not be best interpreted through philosophy or religion, but rather through reality, through observation, lucidity, and reason. To behold this marvelous, intricately conceived world, and then to contemplate the absence of error in creation, leads to a revelation born of a dynamic, intelligible investigation.

How can one argue that such a thing—life, inexplicable in its essence—came by accident and not by design? So long as the denial of a God stems from, and is explained by, chance and nothingness, it remains no more than an inflation of the fatuous. The most vague and hollow of words have been chosen to dismantle the act of creation.

It is not easy to affirm, but it is even harder to argue that God does not exist than to argue that He does. What are the odds that everything, absolutely everything, from atoms to stars, is placed exactly where it must be for life to exist? A calculation that yields a number so vast, it becomes incomprehensible. Even the existence of a single human being is a mathematical absurdity—yet billions have lived. Gravity, radiation, and all the macro-forces of the Universe are distinctly favorable to life. Coincidence cannot reckoning whole. By definition, coincidence is the matching of certain events or elements, a concept that implies limitation. Endless coincidence cannot be handled except through divine touch.

Anyone may doubt anything, they can constantly confront uncertainty. What is known and what remains unknown are both products of premature adaptation. Yet this does not stop anyone from living fully engaged in the only verifiable reality: the present. Observations cannot be achronic; they are privileges of the moment, and whoever loses touch with the present denies the provisional. What one knows today may be replaced, what one discovers may become obsolete. Neither the known nor the unknown has ever shown its complete, final form. Only man, through a kind of nonchalant inspiration, tends to finalize the unfinished through undefined, accessible fragments. He poses the question of truth by slicing into the infinite mystery. A word, a discovery, a theory, all can shake his resolve and tempt him into prematurely issuing a decisive verdict, one perhaps carved from the realm of disappointment.

Thus, theories like evolution become, for some, irrevocable arguments against the concept of creation. Perhaps the most natural conclusion is that one does not exclude the other, but "natural" refers to the purity of nature, not of reason. As rational beings, how can we not wonder how and why we stand as a unique presence among the animal kingdom?

But if humans descend from apes, one must then ask—like a broken version of the chicken-and-egg dilemma—who came first: the man or the woman? Who mated with the apes to bring about humanity? It is implausible that both evolved simultaneously, shared the same space, and were genetically compatible. Implausible, unless, by some miracle, a Creator orchestrated it all.

God reveals Himself in the blink of an eye. He can be seen in every human being, and remains there until the final blink, when life separates from the miracle of existence and the soul departs from the body. Man's dilemma, when he will close his eyes for the last time, is surrendered to Divinity. This surrender offers a profound sense of trust, a reassurance that life is governed by a supreme being. For others, those without faith, it remains an open question, a vanishing into nothingness. In this context, neither the question nor the answer truly matters, but rather the imperceptible, redemptive feeling of believing in something, a belief that unfolds into a clarifying perspective.

The one who believes in nonexistence admires life as a mere accident. The one who believes in the presence of a Creator lives enchanted by providence, from a perspective fertilized by love.

In life, many dilemmas or questions arise that cannot be resolved through realism alone, they can only be interpreted mystically. This grants the non-believer a disadvantage when confronting the weight of existence. He may disregard or ignore such matters, but this evasion, more common among the young, rich in recklessness, loses its effectiveness over time. As age advances and problems accumulate, man is pushed toward accepting a kind of decline from his once rigorous realism. Late faith often arises from a need for consolation, a way to soothe

the unrest that suffering inevitably brings.

All people believe in something. Some are followers of a religious faith, others agnostic, some atheistic, and others, in recent times, devotees of fantastical theories. To distance oneself from religion does not mean to adopt a consistent, irreducible principle of rejecting faith entirely; even one who challenges spiritual traditions, or several of them, still maintains a belief: a belief that others are mistaken, or a belief in one's own imaginative constructs. The difference between a life lived in spiritual union and one lived in conflict with the immaterial is most evident in how one responds to the invitations of suffering. With faith, one passes through the graveyard as a guest. Without it, one becomes a hospitable of abandonment.

No one can truly say that human destiny is summoned to happiness. On the contrary, it is refereed by suffering. Loss cuts deeper than gain, pain penetrates further than pleasure, abandonment stirs more emotion than attachment, absence disturbs more than presence, betrayal leaves a stronger impression than loyalty; life strikes hardest through what is unpleasant. One of religion's regular disciplines is to counter this imbalance in value. Even in endurance, a passion bordering on cruelty, stripped of grace, there is sometimes found a faint expression of a primordial love. For every devout soul, this offers a reason to assign hardship a dynamic cult of sacrifice, a vocation of suffering born from the absurd, unexplained in motive, but which ultimately reveals itself as admiration for what is redemptive.

Endurance draws its strength from Faith. More than that, it is also imagined as a prominent trial. Even without intention, God turns every dead end into a shortcut. What does the lost man in the forest say to himself? The nearest way out is wherever there is light.

Belonging to a religious creed shapes a person. His conduct is steeped in the sacred essence passed down through tradition. One may renounce the culture of their own people upon reaching maturity, but no one can choose the place where their life begins or where their childhood unfolds. Thus, until one breaks from mysticism, they coexist with the victimhood of realism; something that profoundly influences their existence. Language, morality, behavior, attitude, and actions are all framed within the contours of the faith held by the society from which one emerges.

It becomes natural, and often evident, to note the differences in character between two individuals from distinct cultural backgrounds. They respond to one another subjectively, in accordance with their respective educations, sometimes in harmony, often in contradiction, and rarely in full agreement with each other's moral compass. But it is not just perception that differs; their relationship to the material world also shifts: their consumer habits, dress, daily rituals, use of time, and emotional ties to possessions are all marked by spiritual affiliation.

A person's gastronomic preferences are born of tradition—one eats according to one's faith and may regard the food of another as a taboo. The ethics of clothing too are measured through cultural lenses. Daily routines, work rhythms, rest days, and holidays align with religious structure. A society entirely void of spiritual influence does not exist. A freethinker may denounce the present, but cannot erase the past. To cut oneself off from one's roots at the ripening of reason is a kind of spiritual withering.

Atheism, at its core, begins with two assumptions: that the limitless unknown cannot be fully explored, and that absolute truth is inherently inaccessible. More precisely, to deny the existence of a Creator is not a modern rejection of outdated religion, but often a quarrel with the world; a conscious detachment. For without opposition, a man alone on an island could not call himself an atheist. Denial of divinity arises more easily when others are present to challenge, provoke, and be judged.

By nature, humanity is more adept at scrutinizing the errors of others than confronting its own. And no blindness is more common than the refusal to see oneself blunders clearly.

Therefore, disbelief often manifests not from inner conviction, but from disillusionment with the spiritual failures of others. It becomes a form of exile, a retreat from the moral order, caused primarily by critical thinking aimed at one's surroundings. In such cases, even the simplest ancestral ritual may weigh more heavily than the most sublime miracle. Atheism does not stand in the lack of God, but in the deprivation of God.

Moreover, real-world statistics support the notion that the abandonment of faith is profoundly shaped by social context. The distribution is far from uniform; it swells or flattens depending on political systems, educational access, and the moral fiber of a population. Without these societal components, how could one explain why in one country of five million, only 10% identify as atheists, while in a neighboring land of equal population, that number rises to 60%?

If atheism finds virtue in the sincerity of cultural misalignment, a refusal to conform, then religion honors the opposite: it is a disarmament of dissent. One's affiliation to a religious faith is almost always established at birth; conversions are rare. Yet, the specific practices of that faith intensify under environmental pressure. Tradition is learned through the voices of others, not through self-study, and the individual is shaped into a contented conformist, whose primary benefit is the concealment of moral turmoil.

Indeed, religion attempts to elevate morality to a supreme virtue, because, at its core, no faith seeks to teach wrongdoing, at least not those that are recognized and visible. There are indeed cults that revere evil or identify with its spirit, but they are few in number, followers, and visibility. These are generally frequented by those who are innately malevolent; those who are neutral or good are rarely swayed. If all were exposed and visible, human evil would not exist as we know it—because evil, in action, is the visible product of the unseen. The wicked do not manifest malevolence from a place of openness; rather, they cloak it in secrecy or disguise it as good. This very trait marks evil with cowardice and weakness. In a sense, it is almost pitiable.

In whichever direction one traces its path, religion does not lead to a place where evil is cultivated. The journey of faith is one of purification, of confronting and absolving sin. Yet that does not mean that all believers are inherently good, or even capable of such in the depths of their souls. Nor can religion ever eradicate ugliness entirely, it will always persist. For this reason, neither religion nor divinity can rightly be blamed for humanity's failure to conquer its own darker impulses. The issue lies not in the heavens but in the lack of human wisdom, strength, or integrity. The great human folly is to demand from the divine what it does not offer: reward without labor.

A blaming mind becomes a common response when confronted with tragedy—"If God exists, why would He allow this?" It's a bitter question that fuels disbelief. But the Creator is not the executor of every act—He merely authored the laws. He does not bend them to favor or disfavor. A stone may be used to crack a walnut or to shatter a skull; the choice belongs to the hand that wields it.

Another common disgust, a reflection of death within a world otherwise beautiful, emerges in the spectacle of predator and prey. A gruesome scene, both literally and symbolically. Yet such brutality is the price of universal balance: something must end for something else to begin. Nature functions on the principle that the strong outlast the weak. But contrary to popular belief, the lion is not the strongest character in this parable, it is the antelope's companions, those more resilient than the fallen one, who best illustrate this principle.

Humans should take note. The resonance of evil often begins at its lowest pitch, from the weakest point. The most vulnerable individual in any collective mirrors the archetype of the victim. That is why one must remain conscious of the fact that evil prefers the periphery of power. While the center pulses with an unassailable energy, malice waits outside, probing for cracks. Evil does not attack the heart, it lacks the courage. It moves from afar, striking only where it can retreat unchallenged. Thus, it seeks those furthest from strength, invading their perception and bending their reality.

A society that is entirely good or evil will never exist, but a generally atheistic one may eventually emerge as time ferments. This raises a present dilemma: if universal atheism takes hold, will good or evil prevail more? The answer is elusive. In such a scenario, morality would no longer be a standardized whirlwind shared in common, it would likely become an isolated surge, a personal impulse with no echo. This brings a loss in collective resonance, but a gain in individual tone.

A human being may grow more moral than religion prescribes through personal evolution, but may also devolve into corruption. A passion for honesty can silence a conscience that merely learned theft is wrong. Moral habits do arise in the absence of religion, for no one needs a doctrine to tell them envy is harmful, but such clarity only anchors in lucid minds. The disturbed will drift. Without faith, one no longer possesses a map to find shore, nor the trust that the wind blows beneficial in the sails. Thus, navigating integrity becomes a stormier voyage for the less devout. If confused in human virtues, the disoriented avoid capsizing only through the guidance found in preaching.

On a macro scale, religion serves as a safeguard against collective catastrophe. Even within religious societies, there are lost souls, but their numbers remain contained. To claim that atheism can stabilize communal progress is, in essence, to bet on the goodwill of all. To abandon divinity is a solitary act of renouncing one's calling, while to approach it is a collective gesture of co-responsibility. Paradoxically, God appears in solitude and becomes visible in unity. A civilization on the edge of the abyss evokes a singular thought: "It has been forgotten by God." A man struck by fate draws a single counsel: "He must return to God."

Thus, within communities, religion offers a promise of stability. In isolation, atheism introduces uncertainty to equilibrium. Many have confessed to being near complete failure, even on the brink of death, and found that closeness to faith saved them, it revealed a path forward.

At its core, religion expresses positive values in overwhelming proportion, but also reveals certain negatives: interreligious conflict, fanaticism, and at times, a barrier to progress. These are not taught, they emerge from improper, self-serving interpretations. A minor flaw cannot substitute for a truth, no matter how decisive it may seem, so long as the minor does not consume the whole.

When a religion is co-opted to serve a doctrine of war, to mobilize its followers against another society, righteousness becomes veiled. The negative disqualifies the positive, for the truth, guardian of peace, is sidelined, rendered ineffective. This marks a profound deficiency at the heart of some faiths: the inability to fully eliminate the threat of evil. The perfect religion will be the one that, no matter how many and how wicked its followers may be, cannot be weaponized for diabolical ends. Likely, utopian, at best, for they dwell on an outer plane that ties them to absurdity and fails to unbind them from their own animality.

The universe holds within it an element of volume, this we call space, and its very nature ensures that there is always room for everything. Nothing can fill a void to infinity. This principle is rooted in the totality of all things. No person, no society, no culture or art will ever attain the fullness of plenitude. Outside of the finite system, fullness and emptiness are measures of sensation. One only perceives oneself as filled with goodness or devoid of evil; or as knowing everything, or knowing nothing. This law spares not even the religious paradigm. No matter how imbued with virtue a belief system may be, there will always remain space through which evil might slip.

The ambiguity of religion arises from the fact that man stirs both the negative and the positive at once, with polarization often brought to a standstill by temptation. The purpose of a spiritual movement is not to deny or ignore evil, but to purify it. Therefore, the evil that is manifest must be fought, not hidden, and those who reject religious doctrine simply because of the visibility of evil within it, miss the point entirely.

The greatest good a person can do is to hold evil within himself, and the greatest evil is to hoard good only for himself. Life would be sublime if flaws were not transmissible, while virtues were. A recalibration of sharing would envelop the earth in an overwhelming surge of virtue. The consequence of any action is a domino effect: to engage in negativity or positivity is to spark an ambient agitation reflective of its origin. It is more likely that a person responds to evil with equal harm, and to kindness with similar grace. Good and evil are collaborators in a dualistic world. There is no good without a sliver of evil, no evil without a touch of good.

God is beyond this parable. He is neither good nor evil; He is the absolute. For this reason, divinity cannot be interpreted through the lens of moral consequence or cause. He is not to be accused of inaction or disinterest. If God were to erase evil, then good would vanish with it, for without opposition, there is no competition or comparison. It is within man's destiny to decipher the riddle of this world, it lies in his power to ruin it or to refine it. After all, the world was made for him, not for the gods.

Life flows, regardless of the meaning one ascribes to its events. Every good carries some shadow of bad, and vice versa.

All will, in time, be rewarded for their good deeds. Moreover, as a premise, positive people attract one another, just as toxic people do. Never will a truly good soul endure beside a wicked one for long, they repel each other when their energies fail to align. And no one can live wholly isolated in society. We all engage with strangers daily, even in silence. Therefore, it is necessary for the good to draw closer together, for good deeds become a stream nourishing life. Influence flows like a cascade; both benevolent and corrupt. All of it washes over each of us. Life is so insoluble with goodness that it drips it back onto the one who pours it out.

Every religion holds a scale by which it weighs the exploitation of good and evil; thus, human behavior becomes the sole weight pressing down upon the judgment of the absolute. Perhaps the most familiar rendering of this idea is expressed through the duality of Heaven and Hell—two chimerical realms meant to temper the human urge for unrestrained indulgence in the drama of life. On either side, man abstains from devouring the unpredictable and lives as a guest, passing through a fleeting and enigmatic visit we call existence.

He knows the day will come when he will receive an invitation he cannot refuse, an order to return what was never his to keep: the soul. Within the religious vision, the soul is unbound by time or space, suggesting only one fate: that it will wander an eternity within an infinite realm. Life is but a traverse between the end of a beginning and the beginning of an end. Man appears from the unknown, lives through uncertainty, and vanishes into nowhere. Yet for his understanding, the parable of living was unveiled as an overstatement of experience. The thought of final judgment suppresses the notion that life leads nowhere, creates nothing, and dissolves into meaninglessness. God is an obstacle in the way of finding that life is irrelevant. Without faith, the connection between birth and death is tangled in countless knots of existential vacancy. Meaning is the great untying. An interpretation never compromises, it annihilates confusion and reveals value. It is the hidden language of what cannot be explained.

Heaven and Hell arrive as meaning in counter-meaning. Yet eternity spent in these realms of good and evil ignites concern, or even terror, only in those poised near the axis that divides them. A rare soul, untainted by malice, cannot regard judgment as punishment, but rather as a calling. The one flattered by evil, alienated from humanness, rejects mercy and embraces dread. He will feel more at home in terror, unable to comprehend peace.

Thus, for the undecided, Heaven and Hell assign meaning. But if one were to rank them by psychological burden, which would be harder to endure: an eternity in Heaven as an anonymous soul whose good deeds barely outweighed the bad, insufficient to leave a mark, or an eternity in Hell as a novice surrounded by the most monstrous spirits of all time? A casual dabbler in wickedness cannot earn infamy in an abyss haunted by history's darkest. May fate spare the insignificant from that place, for metaphorically, they would spend eternity washing demons' feet.

The mediocre in goodness belongs to moderation; the minor in evil is raised into perturbation. In one realm, irrelevance is permitted; in the other, it is punished. Just as in this life—a life adrift in insignificance invites unrest. No one becomes someone until they leave a mark. This may be why reality often feels closer to the vision of Hell, and more distant from the symbolics of Heaven. In its depth, Heaven stays veiled in mystery, while Hell becomes a transition to a deeper level.

Life, considered through the lens of uniqueness and in correspondence with religious traditions, is often explored as a race, a marathon whose finish line opens into one of two eternal destinations. Yet some religions propose a different resolution for confronting the end—not a linear race, but rather a cycle. This is the mystical concept of reincarnation.

Such a notion may find greater coherence when applied to the world of non-rational creatures, but for the rational animal, man, it implies a relinquishing of uniqueness in the face of eternity. Eternity, without the passion of singularity, recasts life as a mere alliance between soul and matter, unfolding in harmony with nature, far removed from both the privilege and the burden of being an exceptional, unrepeatable accident. What stands in opposition to the idea of recurrence is precisely the exaltation of transience.

Without reason, a uniform life becomes a universally valid dimension in the world of animals; with reason, it is narrowly acceptable in the world of humans. For many, reincarnation evokes the greatest fear related to death. A life lived with the spirit of being a one-time opportunity carries a different weight, measured in meaning, perception, and intensity. The intellect resonates more naturally with the theory of a singular existence, framing life as a remarkable unfolding, not one episode in a recurring series.

Through reincarnation, even death no longer rescues man from time, nor does it offer the stillness of eternal rest. And more troubling still is the thought that one's parents may not be only one's parents, or that a soulmate might continue into a different shared life with someone else. People may divide over which religion most closely approaches the absolute truth, but one thing remains evident: life regarded as a single gift, granted by divine will, aligns more intuitively with the human mind. Whereas life viewed as a repetitive mission, aimed at purification, finds its resonance in the rhythms of nature.

The only moment when man can blame God for intervening in his life is when he meets his soulmate. Everything else is subject to their own will and choices. Divinity may very well abstain from involvement in the material world, but the soul is the Creator's signature on the contract of life—it does not come from this world, nor does it remain in it.

The way souls meet cannot be attributed to mere coincidence or chance; such a union must involve an orchestrator. How else could two people, who spend a lifetime together in love, who say they were made for each other, meet under what appears to be purely circumstantial events? Across the globe, billions of people live in countless places, and society is extremely dynamic. What are the odds that someone meets their soulmate in the same room, on the same street, at the same job, in the same second, or just a step away? Why don't soulmates end up separated across continents? And even if they do, there will be a reason for them to meet. Only God can fracture an infinity of coincidences.

And yet, recklessly, people resist the irrefutable offer. At the same time, the most pronounced form of self-intimidation in the modern human arises when divine signs are ignored. One who fears the details will never fully grasp courage. That moment when someone blindly passes by the radiant spark of a possible love—where the heart shines, but the mind casts a shadow.

Only a vague, rational creature would squander a gifted splendor and, simultaneously, gamble on the futility of brilliance in darkness. When the heart speaks, the mind should be a silent partner, refraining from judgment and simply attending the conversation. Without the power of words, one cannot give value to the whispers of inner delight. The resistance to confirmation, or the self-restraint in allowing oneself to feel fulfilled in a moment's intensity, would not be possible if people stopped dismantling opportunity from its destined moment.

How do they manage such detachment from favorable moments? Either they ignore them, or they deny them. In both cases, the word becomes the deep complication of loss. The chance is wasted either by saying nothing or by saying everything wrong. Sometimes, when the opportune moment arrives, a single spoken word begins a happiness—or brings it to a premature end. When God sends a wave of favor, and man weakens it with words, the realization is chilling: *"how powerful words are"—how they can cancel divine will and repel a splendor meant just for them.*

Religions, like any philosophy, were founded in words. And historically speaking, this has enshrined the word above eras on the scale of endurance. The buildings where sermons were once delivered have collapsed over time, but the teachings have remained ever-present. A good word doesn't crack with time, it will accompany it until the very end. Human relationships, religious cults, or one's connection with the divine are all built on foundations elevated through words.

Communication with the divine conforms to human capacity, it transforms even the most reckless expectations into something absolute. This connection has taken its most delicate form under the name of prayer. Prayer is the first and final step on the staircase of boundless sincerity. Nothing draws more honesty from a person than speaking to God. And in abstract terms, no one would dare to balance such a conversation with lies. Whether it is a plea or a gratitude, prayer guides a person toward the knowledge of their conscience and pure integrity; qualities essential for attaining wisdom. Strip prayer from a wise man, and what remains is merely an intellectual.

Moreover, being a potent dose of sincerity, prayer acts as a stimulant to the mind, it detaches it from insecurity and loneliness, reshapes it with confidence and resilience. The mind reaches a state of clarity where it endures hardships more easily, precisely because solitude is disassembled, because it knows it can rely on a help, even if divine. Those who survived political prisons, having endured torture and unjust condemnation for standing against oppressive regimes, often shared a common trait: they were deeply faithful. In their harrowing stories, prayer was a constant. Or consider the testimonies of those who survived dire situations in the wilderness, they too invoked divinity in their triumph. With such examples, one could rightfully conclude that something within us stimulates neurotransmitters when we attempt to commune with God.

The discipline of faith narrows confusion, softens mental turmoil, and pacifies inner dissonance. It reduces anomalies, tempers panic, and soothes suffering. To begin with, there is no compelling reason why one should not, either in times of need or as a way of being, internalize a belief in a supreme being. Denial is a form of confrontation with the self, and that implies external interference. But why reject the infinite inner benefits of belief merely on the basis of observing outward limitations? It's ungrounded—and it shows that man is a poor negotiator when it comes to the existential offer.

Without the rigor of the spirit, the tyranny of the external world crushes the peace within. Life holds this strange paradox: that man, from a barren premonition, breeds internal refusal through external union. Those who craft philosophies denying the Creator based on surface-level observation either do not understand or simply cannot accept the alluring absurdity of conviction without evidence. After all, evidence is nothing more than an excess of confirmation. And the obsession with verifying everything, with subjects and predicates and proof, raises life's temperature to the fever of absurdity.

That inner warmth, the ecstatic blaze of being alive, ignites when a person senses something is true without having any proof, and time itself begins to honor that intuition. What more could people ask from faith, when it offers everything? Everything, without concrete answers. Yet those who understand the meaning of a poorly formed question, without bias, can distinguish between uncertainty and the unknown. Better to dwell in unknowing with questions than to be lost in bewilderment with the answers. And faith is the only universal-abstract way of bringing life closer to grasping the absolute unknown. If God did not exist, then who would be the clear sign of wisdom?

9

The flavor of life

The mind is like a bowl into which life pours measured doses of liberty, joy, love, success, money, time, or faith, where truth and falsehood are sprinkled together, where illusion stirs with reality. And at the interim end, kneaded with problems, man is left only to taste the flavor of that concoction. What results is marked by absolute uniqueness; no two blends ever match. To live by imitation is to contradict life itself. No one transcends fulfillment by mimicking another's life, forcing it into self-adoption. Authenticity is visibly inscribed in human biology, and equally, it is felt in the quiet necessity of bearing one's own presence. Without a fitting in the realm of the distinct, the self lacks indispensability and forfeits autonomy. To desire to be like others is merely an expression of discontent with oneself. Through imitation, even a triviality may be inflated with false importance, for true value is the brilliance of originality, while borrowed glory is the mask of the counterfeit. And so, what meaning remains for diversity if all is standardized? If man tailors his desires to the patterns of others, what mystery remains to be uncovered? What hunger for love can exist when all love looks the same? There is only one true void of futility in life: to be passionately drawn to its uniqueness. Every rational being must shape a satisfying and familiar solution aligned with their qualities, or flaws, and inevitably, they will come to know gratitude for simply existing. A borrowed flavor, no matter how refined, will always clash with the palate of the imitator, and there will come a moment when everything in life tastes bland or bitter.

Had man not possessed appetite, he would have invented it through conviction. In truth, he shapes it, measures it, and distances it from what is lived, until his thirst for life dissolves, fleeing any attraction to the mere ease of being. The absence of appetite to do signals a final act of pessimism. This does not necessarily mean that optimism is a universal cure for bitterness. Often, optimism conceals rather than heals. To claim all is well, even in the face of the obvious, is to soothe the spirit through reflex, not resolve, through pacification, not transformation, while the vastness of experience tosses the human through every threshold of the unknown.

What meaning remains in life if evil, bitterness, or tragedy are all positively altered? And conversely, if delight and sweetness are soured into negativity? Perhaps only the meaning assigned by subjective vision. That, too, is a departure from objectivity. Both optimism and pessimism are existential pains; each affects the veritable sense. A life grounded in reality can emerge only through equilibrium, through moderation. Optimism is an insufficiency of lie, while pessimism is a surplus of truth. Neither would be faulty if not so often wielded harmfully. When problems arise, optimism struggles not to strengthen the one facing the hardship, but to downplay the hardship itself. Thus, the prevailing mindset becomes, "It will all be fine," a passive hope that delays action, not, "I will overcome this," or, "No adversity can bring me down," which affirm will and resilience. In this way, optimism, misguided, becomes a gentle deceit.

In the opposite case, pessimism, its negative nature is implied by the immediate rejection of any favorable possibility. It's frightening, this brutal surge of mistrust that doesn't merely rush in but explodes into exuberant moments, dragging the mind into a somber tension between inaction and fear. And yet, pessimism can bring certain advantages in specific situations: caution, moderation, hesitation, avoidance—these are crossroads often taken by the less confident. There is one thing the depths of pessimism never bring to the surface: naivety. Something that optimism can swallow quite easily, and sometimes understandably.

A fair point of comparison, perhaps a balance between the two philosophical outlooks, can be found in their practical effect. What real difference is there between the optimist who passively trusts everything will turn out fine, and the pessimist who refuses to act because he believes nothing will? The mental state differs, but in terms of action, in objective reality, they yield the same result: nothing. One abstains from action thinking fate will deliver good on its own, and the other refrains believing doom is inevitable. No matter how noble or solid the mindset, no matter how refined a philosophy may be, without action, the human is inert in the composition of the lived moment.

So it's no secret, no mystery, it's almost banal, that deep

living consists of drawing passion from both favorable and unfavorable circumstances just as they are, without applying a glaze of superficiality. There is no need to falsify the clear image people already hold of what is harmful. Let nonconformity breathe and emit caution, otherwise, it will morph into an obsession with error. Otherwise, what's the point? Why must everything be cloaked in duplicity?

Without an apparent reason, everything harmful becomes strangely tolerable, where acceptance becomes the antidote, not distortion. In such clarity, doubt leaves no stain, scraps of skepticism dry up, and life no longer frightens by mere temptation. As long as one clings to destructive thoughts, they will not be undesirable to the tyranny of abstinence. At its core, in matters of cynicism, a difficult life, marked by lack, hides beneath layers of restraint, surrender, or abstention.

The very fact that life offers no impeccable security is, underlined, one of the emphatic reasons to live. If danger were removed, man would be left without temptation, without the thrill of feeling alive. For indeed, evolution itself teaches us the usefulness of evil. And it teaches something else: that righteousness is relative; only absolute truth truly matters. What is wrong for one being may be right for another. Without this revelation, no one would dare assert superiority over anything bearing dual meaning. By what right does a person invoke sincerity or claim reason when they don't realize that above every lie lies many truths, until the perfect one is reached?

Things are not entirely indispensable from contrast; on the contrary, within every something lies a trace of something else. Even in sweetness, there's a hint of salt; just as in good, a sliver of evil; in despair, a drop of hope; and behind truth, a small shadow of a lie. Since man has no access to the absolute, the unlimited, the perfect, life becomes a series of selections of truths and divisions of lies.

As a simple example, a candy can pass through many categories of truth depending on the perspective. What's the lie? That it's harmless. What's another lie? That it's disgusting. What's the truth? That it's tasty. Another truth? That it's unhealthy. Yet another? That it brings joy when consumed. And the truest truth? That abuse should be avoided. So why, for some, does the fact that it's unhealthy outweigh its momentary delight, or anything else for that matter? In this way, abstinence deprives every individual of pleasure, an avoided pleasure is a missed chance for happiness.

To savor life means to cherish even that which is harmful, unwanted, or "bad." How can one find happiness when seeking only safety? Nothing in this world is purified of harm; everything contains a hint of danger, even love. In the case of candy, as in all similar things, the only truth that truly matters is the one that advises against excess.

Humans are creatures delegated by chaos. Birth, existence, appearance, talents, environment, friendships, loves, children, and ultimately death—all are emanations of chaos: of disorder, lack of structure, and unpredictability. It is utterly impossible to predict destiny, when even procreation cannot be explained. Everything becomes murky when thoughts turn toward the origin of life. No one explains convincingly *why* we exist, *how* we exist, or *what for*. The only acceptable reason is a non-reason: God.

One could rightly consider everything to be accidental, the place of one's birth, the family into which they're born, the gender and physique they're given, the people they meet, the events they experience—everything, ultimately. The entire fabric of existence is accepted, without capacity for conclusion, as either happy or unfortunate accidents, depending on circumstance. The fact that life offers nothing precise is, paradoxically, a precise argument for living. Otherwise, if dominated by exactitude, life would be preordained and stripped of purpose.

Chaos has conditioned humanity throughout history, it has oppressed life and, lacking direction, has driven man into the vitality of the unknown. It has been, and remains, the most vexing accompaniment to the rhythm of existence. Though uncertain in outcome and unclear even in origin, chaos may be both good and bad. People despise it for its uncertainty. From the outset, it's seen as evil. But why should it be? Even the discovery of passionate love may be the result of chaos.

And so, for this imprecision, a remedy had to be conceived. In ages past, a few inspired minds created it: they invented religion. Religious cults were not founded primarily on proving the existence of a Creator, but more so on instituting order, on bringing clarity to purpose, meaning, habit, control, safety, conviction—in sum, as an antidote to chaos.

We've established that the Divine is denied only in defiance, and that the presence of God is best understood through what people most detest: the infinity of the unknown. It is discrepant to hate chaos and love the One who shelters it.

Moving forward, in the modern age, a culture of safety has emerged, a culture of habit, where everything is planned and calculated, and very little is left to chance. From here likely arose the growing estrangement from the Creator, for in its naivety, humanity now considers itself stronger than uncertainty. It believes it can bend unpredictability to its will without any external aid. And to some extent, it has succeeded. But what is the result?

The modern individual lives trapped in routine, in a safety bubble designed to keep danger and probability at bay. In truth, their primary goal has taken root in meticulously planning the future, without any room for fate. They no longer wish to risk everything for anything, or anything for everything, they radiate through the waste of opportunity. And what is wrong with this? Simply what they feel. If all one does is control, plan, repeat, and in parallel eliminate unpredictability, serendipity, the unusual, then why the surprise when life becomes monotonous, dull, devoid of suspense?

Life is a game. And those who always bet on certainty will, without doubt, win no surprises, only expected rewards. Of course, not everyone enjoys surprises, especially the anxious. But like it or not, they are part of the world's miracle, and more often than not, they delight through the influence they carry.

Control is the evasion of beauty, the cowardice to embrace unpredictability, the excuse for transparency, the poison that kills all wonder. Only those who live conditionally hold control in absolute esteem. To control and insure events is to reduce them to familiarity, which in turn makes change detestable in principle; simply because the unknown frightens by not aligning with expectations.

In the past, people were more reserved with certainties. They lived more in suspense, waking with the question, *"What might this day bring?"* Today, for most, days have become uniform in suspense, entirely familiar, almost indistinguishable. One laid upon the next bears only the smallest variations—*if any*.

This repetitive dread is owed, in large part, to the isolation of chaos. Though there are other causes, beyond this, nothing remains that might contain the supreme possibility of reaching extraordinary states. Everything would become ordinary, unworthy of admiration.

Without disorder, in the truest sense of the word, the world would no longer be a birthplace of life's regeneration, but an exile into the untouched stillness of death. Only in the realm of the lifeless does order reign. To live is to consume the complications of chaos.

With the thought of the "butterfly effect" theory, there emerges, within the spirit of the Universe, a kind of symphony of correct mistakes, which systematically obeys the immanent suggestion of nature's chaotic instrument. This theory, for those unfamiliar with it, is based on a hypothesis: a butterfly flapping its wings on one continent creates an air current that might trigger a storm on another continent, thus initiating a chain of events.

The idea that an insect can alter history is reason enough to consider progress detached from grandeur. In other words, a butterfly moving its wings has an impact that sets off instability, alters its environment, while a sleeping elephant, despite its size, remains inert, stable in a vacuum of influence; no matter how big you are, without action, you change nothing.

All human lives exist as a result of primordial details. Perhaps long ago, a man ended up under a tree, delayed because he couldn't find a boot, and his cat had moved it. At that moment, while under the tree, a bird lands on an apple, which falls. The man catches it, eats it, and, dramatically, chokes. After his misfortune, his wife remarries, and from that union, a child is born. That child's descendants may one day number in the hundreds or thousands, but perhaps one of them was different, an inventor, a writer, someone who left a mark on the world.

Would it be wrong to say that all of our lives are different today because, at one point, a cat or a bird changed the course of human history? Who knows? Everything is a disorder.

Ultimately, the obsession with controlling everything may become humanity's final project. Through chaos, God transits through this world. It's His way of keeping everything in order. If you were to create a world, it would be wise to include a system that maintains control without allowing those inside to override it at will. That's what chaos is in our world. For chaos is the "divine boundary"—the threshold between observable reality and unassailable unreality.

There is no other explanation for why truth exists in nature but is regulated in the supernatural. When you look at a forest, you see truth and order, but in its creation, it was shaped by chaos and miracle. Without the "divine boundary" keeping objective reality grounded in regularity, everything would lose its position and value within the perceptible world. Exact order can only exist if absolute disorder is controlled; only the cognizant can surmise Who can do that.

Of course, it would be absurd to suggest life should be lived entirely in a spirit of chaos, but equally flawed is a life governed by obsessive control over events. In a safety bubble, all that is beautiful decays into the ordinary. We need novelty to sustain a continuous expression of ecstasy. Otherwise, in the calm of sameness, routine, and order, and in the fear of change, risk, and disorder, life becomes overloaded with boredom and drained of suspense. This inevitably leads to a perception distorted by ugliness: a symptom of life dysmorphia.

The fear of change, throughout the course of humanity, is

equivalent to never inventing the wheel. Man invented the wheel more for the sake of wandering than for moving forward. It is useless to have the capacity for progress if you place sharp edges on possibility through fear of transformation. No one can travel far in life without being propelled by a stronger force for change.

Replacement, as well as renewal, brings sufficient favor into existence that avoiding trying something new seems not only unwise but flawed. Those who resist change remain parked in an emotional state, in deep-rooted attachments, in a living mindset, all of which serve the cause of stagnation; and nothing can move them beyond a life based solely on what they already have, inherited, or rooted into.

The modern human is a victim of inheritance. It is astonishing how ambitiously and relentlessly the past follows him, ruining his openness to the present or future. It is a kind of envy that seeks to eliminate happiness unanchored by memory or origin. No matter what one does, a person cannot fully escape the inherited burdens — not even through amnesia. They might grit their teeth wishing to erase everything, to restart from an empty point, with no weight, but they can't, not with a desirable outcome.

Inheritance does not refer only to material possessions; it silently collects from every step of existence, every event, every unfolding. It coalesces into one's very way of being. It's sensitive to involuntary assent. History didn't only leave behind tangible traces, it clung to the very structure of humanity: the genetic, the mental.

Thus, behaviors, fears, habits, ideas, abilities, and potential, in general, all that is not freshly born, have been passed down, in some form or another, from generation to generation; entirely or in altered, evolved forms. So why do some people today suffer from fears that no longer represent real danger? Because they inherited them from their ancestors.

For hundreds of generations, humans lived in primitive environments, adapted, survived, and eventually progressed — slowly or rapidly. The tool that crowned this ambition was the brain. It developed in proportion to necessity. Life was primitive; the mind remained in accord with this reality. Everything was in harmony, in mutual understanding, until a point: when some enlightened minds radically evolved life, and the brains of all were caught off guard, still in a primitive stage. The mind must transform alongside external stimuli to balance the interaction. Otherwise, it becomes an obvious handicap, a mute replica of the self.

Adaptation happens—but slowly—and more through mistake and suffering than through ideal and ease. The current civilization is far too advanced for the outdated mentalities of some, and truthfully, this circumstance harms not only those individuals but also society, to a certain extent.

All behaviors of this type: stealing, killing, along with the seven deadly sins—envy, greed, wrath, sloth, pride, lust, gluttony—are primitive emanations, devoid of evolution. Similarly, those cultivated through neurotransmitters—anxiety, fear, behavioral and cognitive disorders, and even lying, perhaps; fall into this same lineage.

These inconveniences were once controlled and managed in the past through various cerebral responses. The brain adapted to the environment in such a way that, given the predictability of a world familiar for centuries, it stimulated a hormonal response efficient enough to domesticate the wildness of negative emotions, and why not, the positive ones too?

Memory does not only reside in images, thoughts, and recollections, it agglutinates genetically, transmitting to future generations mechanisms acquired through living. Today's humans have natural instincts that did not exist 3,000 years ago. Just like now, a child born in a tribe will have different inclinations or natural talents than one born in the middle of a metropolis. Does a young man born into a family of generations of hunters share the same athletic frame as one from a lineage of nobles? Do they run alike? The same goes for intellect.

For centuries, humanity lived in a medieval manner, lacking nonconformity, and then, suddenly, the world shifted into a technological whirlwind. The mind took a shock, it didn't know how to respond to the new impasses. The grandfather lived from agriculture, physical labor, no fixed schedule, enduring hardship, while the grandson woke up in a digital world, with little effort, routine, and a comfortable life.

Some alignments between the mind and the environment have broken. The consciousness was used to hardship, knew how to fight it; not perfectly, but effectively. But suddenly, it found itself in a different world. The idea that life is hard remained, but the tools to deal with hardship became obsolete. Without a valid response, the perception of difficulty became unmanageable, and paradoxically, a better life began to appear worse in the eyes of many. A surge of "life dysmorphia."

This generation seems sacrificial. It's the borderline between two completely different worlds, having inherited outdated habits, behaviors, and mentalities that will mean little in the coming social order. And those who are contemporary with this shift will suffer most, for they are the first to initiate the neurological adaptation for what the next few centuries will bring.

In their time, everything changed with staggering speed. Society shifted from handwritten letters to instant, unlimited, multichannel communication, available in one's pocket—all in just a few years. This isn't an exaggeration of personal victimhood, but a lucid understanding of a phenomenon. Many people wallow in the idea of being circumstantial victims of the times, and this isn't excusable, it's *reproachable*. Worse still, many amplify their inner turmoil through hedonistic distractions, which strip them of the discipline needed to endure suffering with grace.

A medieval man lived between wars. He'd march into battle, through cold and rain, heading toward a potential meeting with death. At home, his family was haunted by famine, disease, and hardship, and yet, he maintained his patience. He didn't lose his composure. Today, someone may become distressed over misplaced keys. Why? Because they've untrained their tolerance. Stress erodes tolerance, just as tolerance erodes stress. It's a relationship like that between assassins: which one kills the other first.

Everything "bad" has a complementary good. Nothing exists entirely in good or evil—only fractions. The brain does not grasp negation naturally. You cannot say, "Don't think about the rain," without immediately invoking a storm in the mind. This is why you shouldn't tell a child, "You're not allowed sweets," but rather offer alternatives. Negation embeds a closed element into consciousness, igniting the urge to open it. Which raises a curious question: Why did God tell Adam, "You must not eat from the tree"? Surely, He knew Adam would break the rule—after all, He created man and knew how he thinks. Was it to have an alibi before humanity, to let them carry the guilt for the birth of death and sin? Controversial, at best.

But what is clear is this: a perfect prison for man is not built on restrictions, but on directions. If a community were to be isolated on an island, the best method of keeping them there wouldn't be to ban escape, forbid boat-building, or erect barriers. That would merely provoke rebellion.

The best approach would be to give them purpose, meaning, a sense of importance and direction. That way, they'd develop habits, attachments, and would never wish to leave. Fences and locks may work on individuals, but at a collective level, a fence becomes a problem. Its mere presence multiplies attempts to escape. People start asking, "Why are we being kept here? What lies beyond it?"

A sense of conspiracy always seeps in when an obstacle is both obvious and poorly explained. Even a massive, meaningless boulder placed near a human settlement would be ascribed meaning by those living nearby. They'd obsessively search for a reason, a story, a secret behind it.

Thus, humans have inherited a remarkable brain, yet one still lagging behind the explosive evolution of society. But it will adapt, inevitably, to the new standards. It will develop new mechanisms to digest overwhelming emotional stimuli. Today's world is made up of minds configured and clenched within an inept consumption, bombarded by a glut of craving events. The supply not only exceeds demand, it exceeds curiosity, comfort, and capacity. A man can be the laziest of all beings and still experience amusement from a couch. What once required minimal effort is now delivered instantly. At the same time, curiosity fades, everything arrives at his doorstep.

Will he manage to coexist with monotony without greeting madness, without losing his mind? That remains to be seen.

Naturally, consciousness should evolve and pull him out of this tasteless existence. Consumption without appetite will eventually inspire an obsolete meaning. True, some might deny the direction of evolution, it doesn't make itself obvious. It seems, on the contrary, that people are regressing, relying more on primitive instincts. More envy, hatred, deceit, greed; a valid observation. But this is explained by the inexplicable. It's like a teenager who was kept away from socializing and, when finally invited to their first party, gets drunk, loses control; an erratic outburst. Society is undergoing a similar transformation. It came from a closed, outdated, restricted world, and when it crossed the threshold into an open, vast, modern one, all restraints collapsed. But it's a phase, things will settle eventually. Primitivism will adjust to the new life. Without question, this current generation remains one of sacrifice, a transitional bridge between two vastly different worlds.

To live caught between a mediocre mind and a weakened body is not inevitable, it is unpardonable. Weakness can only be a testament, seasoned by remnants of vitality, handed over to destiny with the duty of dissolving man in an existential struggle.

Every tolerance that harnesses weakness willingly invites a vital resentment and brings with it a whisper of mortality. Without strength, life dulls into a competent disgrace of being, a failure so justified that it practically demands to strip man of his right to fulfillment.

Life breathes through the endurance of suffering, and

through the maturing of vitality, man eventually learns to believe in someone far removed from weakness: himself. Suffering is not just a reality, it can be both recipe and preparation. It is an indispensable ingredient in the flavor of life. And thus, deciding how you taste it becomes a fundamental meaning of existence, one that is discernible. A strong man has endured pain, either by choice or by circumstance. A weak one, on the other hand, will inevitably be forced into torment.

Thus, one of the most important decisions in life lies in how a person chooses to face suffering. Either through discipline, voluntarily, which strengthens their inner power, or through shock, as a result, a backlash from weakness. In one case, pain appears at the beginning, while in the other, at the end. In one, it's controlled by order, in the other, triggered by chaos.

However, what matters most isn't the direction or the source, but the intensity. Ordered, balanced suffering is bearable and manageable. Sudden suffering, as a reaction, is brutal and destructive, it's far harder to contain.

It's important not to judge things by appearances, because sometimes, something small causes more damage than something big. Think of a sheet of glass lying on the floor, and over it walk a woman in high heels and an elephant. Although their weights are vastly different, when the woman steps on the glass, it's far more likely to shatter under the concentrated pressure of her heel. On the other hand, when the elephant walks across, the outcome is less predictable. For this comes down to a basic law of physics: the heel has a small surface area, which concentrates all the force on a tiny point. The glass undergoes intense stress and shatters. The elephant's broad foot spreads out the force, reducing pressure per square inch, and thus, the glass might endure.

That's how pain manifests in life. Suffering that comes suddenly, as a consequence of weakness, is like the heel: sharp, crushing, destructive. Suffering that stretches gradually from the start, as a chosen hardship, is like the elephant's foot: heavy but tolerable, spread out in a way the mind can handle.

An expedient frames existence in balance. Though not the most illuminated of priorities, it gleams brightest in the darkest hours, when hope and meaning are absent, and the spark that ignites self-transcendence threatens to fade. Meaning arises of itself, purpose from meaning, reason from purpose, and destiny from reason. All is interconnected. Yet it is that very "self", the primal elixir, that sets this chain of causality in motion. Like an alchemist blending essences in search of a pure, radiant, incorruptible substance that mixes life with purpose.

An elixir lacking its vital ingredients—strength, learning, trust—will inevitably yield a fate deceptively unjust. Here too, the formula flows in reverse: Trust begins with the self, upskill from trust, and power stems from skills. Everything revolves around the self; it is the original source of light. Man is the center of his own universe; the world revolves around him, not the other way around. He gets *nowhere* step by step, for he gets lost in abstraction, for *somewhere* is a destination that arrives "idea by idea."

If the mind is an elevator, then a step on the stairs becomes a stunt. Without breath from thought, feeling and intuition would suffocate. Therefore, the mind is the primordial force, arrogantly proud when it exports authenticity into mediocrity. Likewise, to live authentically demands a dramatic and visceral battle with weakness, for once weakness is conquered, the emptiness within all things collapses.

The weak do not cherish others, nor themselves; they become a contagious presence, a contemplative agent of betrayal. And what more can be said? That a man whose back is full of scars has surely had many weak friends. The strong speak plainly; they strike in daylight. The malicious operate hidden; because they are, by nature, weak.

This isn't just true of friendship, it extends to love. If love is not strong, it will succumb to trials and fall to temptation. Shock severs what is fragile, as was said before. And likewise, fulfillment too is derailed by weakness on its journey toward becoming real. Success moves with upward inertia, but that alone does not carry it to the summit, it demands extra force. If achievement is not continuously pushed forward, it slides backward into the valley of failure. Without cultivating strength, man abandons his role in the world, lapsing into a kind of existential unemployment—irrelevant and adrift. All of life is tested by weakness, every aspect, experience, and event. Nothing escapes it.

Yet perhaps the most catastrophic pairing occurs when trembling hands grasp the most potent social tool: money. If the weak are intelligent, but lack fortitude, they'll descend into madness, for madness assumes the presence of a mind. (As a side note, foolishness seems to immunize against madness.) But if they are neither strong nor intelligent, they'll spiral into an inflexible relationship with well-defined stupidity.

For the sake of peaceful living, such flaws are best left to the will of destiny. Otherwise, if taken on as self-blame with too much force, one ends up in a cruel dead-end, gripped by negligence and a fierce hatred for the self. Being overly harsh, condemning oneself daily, leads not to growth, but self-torture. A cycle of self-blame is a common cause of chronic sadness.

All people can be strong, but not everyone is fit for strength, some find solace in weakness. What matters most is a cordial effect of good and beauty, and how it's attained is up to each individual's path. If one's intuition whispers that strength is not their route, then the correct alternative is to take responsibility for their fragility. Don't leap across a weakened bridge.

Of course, the discourse has extensively addressed the importance of gaining strength and the damage wrought by weakness. Yet, by its close, an apparent contradiction emerges, an exception, but the prevailing reality still leaves space for interpretation. What remains just, in the end, is that the flavors of life should not be tainted with bitterness; its savor should be rich and pleasing. Even the strongest can fall into disillusionment, may develop an existential dysmorphia, but without committing a sin in saying so, it is far less likely for them than for the weak—a truth both prevalent and consequential.

Life, at its core, is a weaving of power: power unexploited makes you your own slave; power harnessed makes you your own master. While acquiring strength, both physical and mental, is undeniably encoded in the decryption of destiny's mysteries, one must also possess the ability to direct and wield it. Without this, power spirals erratically, drifting toward the edges of selfhood.

What becomes of a man who has vitality and intellectual capacity, yet lacks the knowledge to apply it toward his own ends? He becomes a tool, useful to others, but indistinct himself, a permanent servant in life's unfolding. Power is like ink: it can be used to stamp another's dream, or to write your own story. Without autonomy, without freedom of thought, even the mightiest force loses its luster; the ornament of strength dulls. Only through articulated self-command does power become a tool that fills the haunting void of meaninglessness. Unsettling, for it is unvoiding how man can only be filled by blanks. For all else, he has infinite space, yet trivialities crowd him quickly, compressing his potential.

Thus, the evacuation of the irrelevant is necessary, to free the self from the tyranny of limitation. Without this retreat into void, life's charm would slide along a straight line toward one meek target: infinity. Otherwise, the collision with reality's edge is brutal.

In notionally terms, true cleverness lies in architecting life through reverse engineering. One must fix the endpoint: boundlessness. With that destination set, the person shapes their progress unconditionally. If one starts from the beginning rather than the end, all is seen from behind. Why? Because the world is already in motion, everything is far from origin, and any beginning is burdened with the tedium of its own deficiency.

To walk in another's footsteps doesn't teach you to surpass any noble ideal; it leads instead to a mimicry of distortion. It wouldn't be so unforgivable if people didn't feel offended when overtaken, especially if they truly knew where they were going. But in truth, you cannot reach excellence by mimicking the neighbor's stride. More than that, excellence itself becomes trivialized, epigrammatic, for any borrowed identity will be the subject of fate's own satire.

Only through an immaculate, resolute, even unyielding stance does one gain the aura that repels irony, a stature worthy of true respect. And to reach this state, a person must legitimize their power, becoming a distinguished master of it, a unique soul with the skill to lunge like a vampire toward the anemia of creation.

Every achievement comes after a bleeding of chances, and strength is the balm that seals every wound; protecting the self from infection by misplaced devotion. Yet, power is not without recoil, it can also inflict harm. It does not only aim to strike precise targets. A feeling of power can birth malicious sentiments: envy, contempt, wrath, scorn; anything that disturbs well-being.

Thus, for the one who treads in another's footsteps, it is self-evident that he must never prick, or give even the impression of pricking, anyone other than the one he follows: the mentor. Even if, in the depth of his being, he senses himself more capable, more vigorous, or more intelligent, it becomes imperative that he does not reveal it; lest he invite danger. Let the mind advance quietly while actions and words remain behind, or at the very least, concealed. This is pure wisdom: the prudence of restrained power.

He who fails to grasp this principle will fashion many rivals. And the most perilous of enemies are always born from the familiar. Resentment does not come from afar, but from colleagues, relatives, friends, neighbors; even, unthinkably, from parents. If you wish to forget loyalty, just remember your friends.

What unites them all? The subtle power they hold over you. If they carry hatred in their hearts and are capable of harm, make no mistake, they will deliver it. That is why a life that begins from behind, seeing everything in retrospect, learns early to let go of ego, for pride will summon battles that were never meant to be fought.

This is why, throughout life, one often meets individuals with influence, people who do not seek to relinquish power, but to tame it, to mold the world into followers. It is a strategy of interest. And in order to reach a favorable position, the apprentice must cultivate the art of elegance in power; and, in time, learn to wield it with refinement. If not, he will inevitably meet deviation.

The influential is not always the most intelligent or strongest, but more often an opportunist blessed by timing. Success does not favor brilliance alone, the highest stake is self-trust. Life is played out on the table of time, and all advancement rests on making decisive moves at the right moment. Otherwise, when the clock is reviewed out of sync, two ghosts of lost momentum rise: *"too soon"* and *"too late."*

The aroma of time presses against the moment, and disregarding that pressure causes every stretch of duration to dissolve into fragments of failure. To labor under time's weight is not to look forward or backward, but within the laborer. Pressure generates resistance, and it is through this current that power flows. From within, the essence of timing is born; a necessity to infuse life's every preparation with the flavor it deserves. Because some flavors only remain ripe in their proper season.

Money, love, or success do not escape the influence of timing, they merely stage the whims or despairs of life. They cannot transcend it, for what comes too early is unripe, and what arrives too late is spoiled. Thus, the true weapon of power lies suspended between patience and riposte. Action must not be impulsive, triggered by the first temptation, but neither lost in endless waiting, fading at the last opportunity.

Otherwise, the "flavor of life" loses that bewitching and intense taste it only offers at its proper moment; in its rightful time. And so, more briefly put, this is how the power to command time directly reflects in one's life. Yet, there are ways to work with time indirectly, through the virtue of experience.

Returning to the topic of mentors and progressing along others' paths, it's worth underlining that those who are further ahead, more engaged in their journey, have consumed far more moments. Not only that, but they also bear an older age, which often signals a handover of initiative. This condition can be strategically exploited by novices, through aptitude for power, with the purpose of equipping their own capacity. How? In a manner of no particular manner, by exploiting the greatest vulnerability of those in positions of power: their love of advising.

People love to give advice. From the lowest failure to the highest achiever, all are enchanted by the act of guiding others. The reason is simple, almost intuitive: giving advice feeds a person's sense of importance, of being heard, of feeling superior. And why is this a weakness? Because it can be exploited by the intelligent. Not only do advisors give away meaningful insights for free, knowledge they acquired over time, but even when the advice is useless, they still suffer a subtle erosion of influence. Why? Because they cede time and attention to the listener. In doing so, they lose a bit of power, and the one who listens gains.

Contrary to what many believe, giving advice does not elevate the advisor further into superiority; on the contrary, it raises the recipient into significance. Hence, a refined source of power lies in the ability to draw attention, and the most elegant method is precisely this: leveraging humanity's passion for advising.

In the end, whether the advice is good or bad is irrelevant, what matters is the attention it attracts. And in this somewhat cynical way, one may flavor the essence of life using the borrowed time of others.

Still, there remains one more valuable truth to mention: that even bad advice, when truly good, can arise from within oneself. Give yourself foolish counsel and learn through folly. It is a pure and innocent method of building strength through the experience of error. After all, a controlled mistake is an open wound upon the conscience, healing itself with knowledge.

Thus, one proceeds further, descending into the heart of error, where even illusions cannot rival the rapture born of confronting one's own recklessness. Prudence, in the end, is educated through mistake, whether voluntary or not. In retrospect, every error is a predication, and when repeated, it becomes an application.

Much like the model of "questions and answers," in which posing a question to oneself reveals part of the response, so too with deliberate mistakes: a similar principle holds. The most profound scene of personal transformation, of human evolution, is the one in which a person plays all three roles at once: the accused, the accuser, and the witness. And at the end of the act, they do not emerge as the same actor, but as a new character, one capable of understanding them all.

Mistake is not the fruit of weakness, but the graft from which power grows. Only the withered man is infallible, for once faded, he no longer has the freshness to grow anything at all.

And what more could be said? That self-condemnation for error is senseless, a mere pretense for impression, a means of robbing oneself of innocent freedom, no matter the direction.

Error is the source of human existence. It is what allows us to appreciate the quality of creation. It is life's integration point, and all need it, lest they fall into disintegration through idiocy. For it enlightens, transforms, corrects, and refines all that had not existed before its occurrence. Is there any path toward development that does not pass through improvement? Unlikely. Thus, to feel a virginal passion for error is merely a form of shyness toward the love of deed.

So then, why condemn yourself when you could overcome yourself? Sit still. Reflect. Grit your teeth until the dentist marvels. Clench your fist until your nails wound your skin. Descend into the deepest abyss of transfiguration, and from there, with ruthless will, defeat the destructive self, annihilate its harmful influence, and, in the end, let what remains be a character fierce in resistance, unshakable in form. And only in this way can the fear of failure and the audacity to seek perfection avoid dragging the individual into the peril of doubt. To strive for perfection is, in truth, an ideal mistake.

Self-interest is one thing, but the common interest is a magnetic force, it either attracts or cancels out rejection, depending on its alignment with the reality of profitability. It depends on the polarization of sensation in its phase. This is how relationships begin, and how they separate. All human connections have a knot signifying a benefit, a shared advantage, because no one truly embraces the lie of attachment unless they perceive some satisfaction of their own needs.

No person bonds with another based on the recommendation of nothingness. Simply put, emptiness does not suggest unity; it confirms incompatibility. Perhaps one could argue that the study of human relationships would give even the most brilliant thinkers a headache; intelligence would strain itself trying to grasp how people interpret and calculate "nothing", especially when they assess someone's relevance to their own interest.

Nonexistence is complementary to the existence of information. Which, paradoxically, explains why people often compose great weight out of nothing when evaluating someone's importance. And yet, it remains puzzling why individuals are quick to spot the emptiness in others, but not in themselves. Could it be that emptiness takes form only when it proposes itself as a factor of connection, or disconnection? No one detaches from themselves without losing adhesion to life, which would then be replaced by an attraction toward nothingness.

In any case, potential is usually overlooked when judging someone, as people tend to focus on what that person already has and what they can presently offer. Undeniably, this is a flaw of power, because in perspective, over time, ascension outweighs stagnation, and those who choose what *is* over what *could be,* end up opting for a lesser benefit. Therefore, bad decisions are underestimations of the future, and this in turn spoils the taste of life—its very flavor grows bitter.

Love, happiness, success, money, even freedom—none of these turn a blind eye to poor choices. And it's a good thing they don't. Otherwise, life would be built on visible blindness, a way of living that drifts into dead ends. The fact that some people don't choose out of fear of making mistakes, that alone is reason enough to liken the human race to an overabundance of circumspection.

The power of choice is, at its core, a fundamental existential principle—the foundation upon which all empires of nothingness crumble, giving way to the formation of a kingdom of meaning. Man guides his life through decisions; he is a confused sovereign, endlessly seeking, within his world, a throne welded in purpose. He either endures in anticipation of materialization or lunges toward illusion; in both scenarios, the decision acts as a servant, and the benefit plays the fool.

Of course, this isn't mandatory, but without it, one no longer builds a fortress, but instead lives as an existential nomad. However, by far, the greatest challenge lies in maintaining the citadel of life intact, without allowing it to be trampled by enemies.

With each brick laid, man becomes increasingly valuable to those eager for conquest, or to opportunists. Success and money, specifically, best attract the invasion of the immoral. Those devoid of morality are never short on cunning; they are normal in betrayal and abnormal in integrity. And their method of operation is simple, covert, and most tragically effective: through friendship. Obviously, betrayal is a privilege granted through alliance, understanding, and trust.

How would history have looked without betrayal? From the smallest tribe to the largest empire, betrayal has been felt and recorded. Some historians may argue that certain wars ended more quickly because of betrayal, but that only highlights the obsolescence of interest; a lesser or outdated interest cannot resist a newer, stronger one.

Thus, the power to control both interest and its consequences is essential in preventing a descent into ruin. A man should not sell water to the thirsty, doing so quenches a future enemy. He must, instead, compensate that thirst with an interest cloaked in goodwill; a potential friend must repay their debt. No one truly befriends to sell necessity, but to lend against need. And when one finds themselves in such a position, with the world forever captivated by the supply of demand, a sacrifice of renunciation becomes imperative. A renunciation of expectations, of anything that might replace satisfaction with disappointment. Dissatisfactions must be swallowed like hot tea: while they are still warm and the air is cold. If not, time will make sure to spill them into frustration.

There is no depth in letting go without dissatisfaction, just as, generally, there is no renunciation without profound satisfaction. A distanced man has either separated fulfillment from need, or detached interest from necessity. How could a bond be maintained if one is dissatisfied with what they need? Or how could it exist if one is disinterested in what is necessary? The fundamental utility of a long-term relationship lies in the courage to close one's eyes to the fear of uselessness. That would be the natural order, but it rarely is. Because no one can endlessly overlook the exposure of what is useless. If everyone managed to, the world would descend into a paradoxical salvation: everything depends on nothing. What purpose would a life without meaning still have? Is not the only absolute reality the one born of significance? Only illusion confuses the lacking with the unlacking.

For this reason, existence carries both interest and necessity through meaning, and life implies admitting consequence as a release of condition. Two former colleagues are no longer friends because one changed jobs. It's simple: the condition of friendship was being coworkers; the consequence is disconnection. Two former business partners part ways when the company collapses—again, easy to explain: the foundation was financial, the outcome is dissolution. And so on...

But while the reasons may be simple, enduring them is

far more complex. A sufficient dose of strength is needed to accept surrender. Otherwise, if life is not furnished by agreement, its interior will remain unfitting, hosting a dreadful rift. If someone enters a disordered, deplorable home, will they care not to make a mess? Clearly, no. But if they enter an immaculate home, they will take great care not to leave a dirty mark. Such is the way people "visit" a life—if it inspires no decency, cleanliness, or clarity, its guests will be ugliness, misfortune, or harm. And as a result, existential dysmorphia knocks at the door.

Undoubtedly, the power to govern both interest and acceptance is a form of orchestration. And whoever manages it becomes a tamer of impasses. Even more, they become a trainer putting on performances of tolerance. Yet at times, there are issues that seem impenetrable, hard to bear; especially those rooted in familial equations.

Relationships born of money, gain, advantage are easy to form, almost instinctive, and just as easy to surpass in separation; the parity remains from entry to exit. But naturally formed bonds—through blood, birth, location, emotion, coincidence—cannot be dismissed so easily. They bring acute suffering when ruptured. Why is it different? Because man does not control the entrance, it is in the hands of fate, of chaos, and thus he gains no knowledge of the exit's parity. The tragedy deepens even more when one realizes that often, a personal misfortune brings the greatest satisfaction to those closest, family and friends.

Envy appeared in the world with the first two brothers, and without doubt, it will remain until the last. This sentiment of hatred is a mark of familiarity; envy of strangers is no longer envy, it is mere repulsion. More disproportionate than inequality, hatred reigns supreme in its irreducibility.

Essentially, man falls from grace through sympathy, with disdain or indifference, but never out of spite. Once fallen from someone's favor, nothing can truly mask the detachment from indifference, and with each occasion of interaction, the individual emits a hysterical force that digs into memory. He calls to recollections when whispering pleas for sentimental repair. In vain. Without success, all he hears is a busy tone.

Meanwhile, in a realm far removed from impassivity, more precisely, somewhere suspended between obsession and premise, dwells the sentiment of enmity. The bisector that separates sympathy from hostility is memory; it is the shared edge that forges two planes that seem so close, yet remain so distant. In the fall from grace, the fallen one is wounded, eager to reconcile, and ignored. Conversely, in the rise to hatred, the one elevated to scorn stands in the opposite posture: he ignores, seeks no reconciliation, and feels no sorrow. The emotion is reversed.

When a person hates, envies, they induce suffering and a morbid attachment toward someone; evidently, a form of irrational self-torture. When someone allows themselves to be affected by a remorse for lost grace, they too cause suffering and an unhealthy attachment, but this is a rational torment, typically grounded in the awareness of having erred, in a sincere regret. Eternal regret is shared with a single second of guilt.

Therefore, to avoid psychic pain, never offer hatred, nor beg for sympathy, always spin gracefully around the mention of either.

Yet, what is envy, beyond its recognition as a sin? How does it reflect and rebound within the vault of one's own inner peace, bypassing lucidity? Envy is reality corrupted by the integrity of illusion. That is, it is a true emotion, wrong and destructive, but masquerades as a concrete falsehood within the mind's capacity to perceive what is real. It would not wound the conscience unless the mind was already obscured by shadow. It can manifest as a mere habit, in which case, it becomes frequent and dismal. Or, it can arise as an exception, in which case it resembles a "spiritual adultery."

The soul marries truth once it has crossed beyond the boundaries of vagueness. Thus, envy thrives at the base of the social pyramid, where people lack moral integrity unless they break ranks from the confused modesty of that structure. In concrete terms, an individual who endlessly denounces grandiosity has likely been eclipsed by the refracted brilliance glimpsed in darkness. Hatred radiates only where the presence of a significant figure among the insignificant feels excessive. As one ascends the social pyramid, mediocrity becomes the exception, until at the peak, it is entirely renounced; a fact that nullifies hatred in its purest form.

Absolute fraternity, founded on respect and trust, untouched by envy or betrayal, can only be forged in the complete absence of even the faintest strands of dark thoughts, in that rare place, at the pinnacle of a mind fully illuminated, refined through inner edification. Thus, hatred is natural among the familiar, among those dwelling in the comfortable obscurity of equality, for any small spark of personal progress disturbs the calm of collective stagnation. Equally natural is the way distance from such familiarity inspires a sense of individual reverie. More precisely, a person becomes increasingly attuned to their inner self when no longer enveloped by the toxic haze of others — feeling instead a subtle breeze stirred by the fragrances of their own life.

And yet, how easily the unknown tempts, and how difficult it is to separate from the known. For every redirection belongs to the realm of power, where weakness shields emotions, while power strips them of privilege. Accordingly, envy emerges as a primordial sin born of weakness, and escape from it comes only through the fierceness of strength. Of course, only with resolve can one make vital decisions, those of change or expansion. Were it otherwise, what meaning would the desire to break free from attachment still hold, if all could be released by nothing more than the softened reasoning of a weakened mind?

He who seeks transformation has first been revealed in disappointment, through a lucid and persevering clarity. And with each revelatory detail, man undergoes a mental metamorphosis, trivializing the old self, and impersonating a new character; one that steadily dulls the primitive instinct.

At first glance, one might perceive a tendency to lead the individual toward the mysteries of knowledge, away from barbarism. Yet what remains unintelligible to him is revealed in the inner revolt that arises when the beast within is wounded; when instinct is tamed by reason. The lion does not know it is a "hunter," and therein lies a tribute to nature itself. The animal's mind does not question the food chain; it does not pause to ask, "Why must I kill?"—only "How must I kill?"

Now, if man becomes aware that he is a hunter, what changes? Everything. He subjugates the expression of nature through all that emanates from the mind, reaching a truce with a kind of passivity praised by inertia. More plainly: through morality, justification, consequence, mercy, or other human constructs, instinct does not vanish, it is merely restrained. Certainly, some might argue that the act of killing an animal is primitive, and human evolution lends weight to this claim. Yet what deserves even closer scrutiny are the instincts that do not inspire ugliness, but aspire to beauty, such as love.

One may argue endlessly that it takes strength to take a life and also strength to spare it, a progressive kind of strength. Each person will define strength and weakness in their own way. But how should we judge love that arrives naturally? With questions similar to those asked of the hunter: "Why?", "For what purpose?", "In what manner?", "How?", "What if?", and so on. The subject changes, the answers differ, yet the algorithm of judgment is the same. It's a programming of thought that, in certain circumstances, generates a logical error, an execution fault caused by a failure in emotional processing.

More poetically put: the brain misleads the heart, detouring it from its refuge in rapture.

Perhaps the costliest mistake a person makes in life is the one they're bribed into most cheaply, the one that impoverishes inspiration from love. He walks, stops, looks, encounters someone, and deep within his heart, he feels something, something special, something inexplicable. And yet, he ignores it. Moves on. As if nothing had stirred him. A common scenario in today's world. Even more standardized is the way people experience love now, engineered through linear simplicity, stretched over time, stripped of spontaneity.

True love is not a straight line with a start and end point; it is a loop, lived over and over again with the intensity of ecstasy. It restarts without warning; it doesn't end on schedule. It can only be broken, abruptly, by death or by something equally unforeseen.

One of the most brutal paradoxes of this world, one for which people suffer, is that they instinctively mix the instinctual with the improvisation of reason. Instinct is not a talent of the brain; it is defined as a congenital, unconditional complex—in other words, reasoning distorts it from its root and makes it deceptive. To develop a strong mind, capable of critical argument, firmly grounded in lucidity and mental effort, is, in certain circumstances, a double-edged sword.

There is the risk of injuring one's own perception of life, but only after it has been shaped through nothing other than the dissecting thought that questions every accompanying element of existence. Reason is a beast, it takes strength to pullulate it, but even greater strength to dominate it. That is something to remember. If one lets it loose, without an imperative grip, it will wreak havoc on life, it will devour every primitive joy. It is what it is: the control of power must be conquered, and the conquest of power must be controlled.

Thus, every existential detail is anchored in an objective force, wandering through the dread of subjectivism, day and night, and if nothing remained of a reality independent of the inessential, then a new world would be born, one refined by biased words and thoroughly delusional thoughts, in which the pack of humanity would chase the necessity of forgetting, erasing the memories of those who once wrapped life in impartiality, for everything would become nothing more than an experience shaped by an access to ignorance, where the daring appear as amateurs, and the conformists sit helpless, witnessing the sprint of their own disappointments—a fact that, to the humble shame of all, leads existence toward the irreparable fantasy of unreality.

Memory, in this context, becomes a right, earned by transposing external experiences into consciousness. It arrives like a wave of potential from a boiling recognition, for through the effervescence of inner life, the fluidity of memory murmurs toward a life in which the void never swells to fill the space.

Formally, any memory is a voluptuousness of the mind, and any forgetting is a malfunction of consciousness. One can never be too cautious in managing forgetfulness, yet it remains a reflex that influences the awareness of consciousness. Out of fear of forgetting, man cultivates a restlessness born from the structure of interest. For the difference between forgetting and remembering is defined by the weight of one's concern. Only light and reactive contradictions of feelings transform memory into a stable inspiration.

Unfortunately, in this world, what has been learned is forgotten like a breeze, while remembering lessons strikes like a storm. The commemorative conception of life stirs an interior tempest that disrupts the calm of existence, once disturbed, it pulls the individual into a harsh whirlwind of experiential reckoning. Nothing honors memory more than the stimuli grounded in reality. In a life of illusion, plagued by the malady of superficiality, memory becomes tied to desperation, to the lack of resilience in the face of renunciation. In this case, memory does not prioritize the recollection of what has been lived, but of what has not.

With that being said, and with all due respect, one might conclude that uncontrolled reason crystallizes like a narcotic that assaults genuine particularities, those that belong to the present or the past, especially those tied to perception or recollection. Everything takes on a farcical air when it is no longer noticed that reality is irreplaceable in the sacrifice of living, because to truly live completes a respect for the abandonment of illusion. With reverence, one attends the ceremony of layered moments, time's thawing occurs through a state of wakefulness blended with a passion for reflection. Unimaginable is a life lived without the power of veneration, for it is the man baited by disregard who reveals himself as one who knows not devotion; who bears no respectful esteem for anything or anyone.

Each flavor of life demands attention and reverence, so that the individual might awaken from the numbness of disregard—the kind that leaves one living dulled by denial. Love, freedom, happiness, wealth, success, or faith—all lay claim to a form of strength born from respect. It is a fundamental requirement; without it, the savor of life emits neither enthusiasm nor, even less, pleasure.

Moreover, self-respect is absolutely essential in any endeavor that calls for passion. What happens when a participant lacks respect for their opponent? The likelihood of blunder increases. In the game of life, the opponent is none other than the player himself. If a man does not respect himself, missteps lurk behind every move. What is most visible in one who has failed monumentally? A profound absence of self-trust and self-regard.

That is why the first round in anyone's life, and arguably the most crucial, is the victory over one's own disbelief and self-disdain. This triumph must be resounding and humbling, so that the old self may not pass on to the next stage but retreat instead into the anonymity of oblivion. Otherwise, if allowed to continue in the existential competition, it relegates the person to the league of the defeated, where the only solemn virtue that remains is the endurance of suffering.

Life restarts with every awakening, with every personal

victory. And each time, the game becomes more complex, more captivating, and more worthy of pursuit. In the vicinity of one's devotions, a person either finds a career in fulfillment, or an occupation in inconsistency. Weak consistency often reveals itself as the offspring of doubt, typically nourished by external comparison. Not everything or everyone deserves respect and value, and those who fail to recognize this in time fall into the trap of misplaced reverence; eventually succumbing to a saturation of hesitation.

That everything is subject to attachment is a certainty. That all things are fleeting, subtle vanishments—this too is beyond question. But one thing remains unclear: that man has no choice. The vitality of decision-making mimics the backlash of chaos; it ends a barren waiting and, along a scale of near-total monotony, a single choice becomes a step climbed toward moments of genuine convergence.

Choice is among the rare faculties of reverse engineering granted to the human race, alongside imagination and anxiety, because it begins at the end, from what is desired, from what chaos would deliver were it not disturbed by the individual's interference. Yet this only holds true when choices are not born from impulse, but from deliberate analysis. That is why they are so difficult to bear and to fulfill, because man wishes to understand why he chose before he chooses. He longs to be the oracle of his own life, yet succeeds only in being a chatterbox.

In the end, every choice arrives with either regret, sorrow, or consolation, or with fulfillment, joy, or satisfaction. For this reason, indecision lingers like a fog over all supposition; hesitation casts doubt on action itself. And nothing can land in the domain of truth, in the real knowledge of outer life, when decisive moments are rare.

Perhaps choices would be trivial matters if they did not risk plunging one into suffering, a suffering that, without doubt, is life's great intimidator. Yet in truth, it is not pain that weighs most heavily on the scale of a decision, but the singular direction of time: its impossibility to reverse, the permanence of a misstep once it's lived. Hence the sorrow that time lends to existence, a sorrow born of irrevocability. Take, for instance, a relationship: once a feeling of love has been experienced, its collapse can stem either from a final cause or an ill-chosen beginning; never from a timeless void. And what deepens the pain is that, in the context of time, the moment to choose again has expired.

The only apparent escape from this fate lies in indecision or in making the right choice. Perhaps no decision will fully prevent suffering—but indecision, too, leaves the soul vulnerable, punctured and exposed to other types of sorrow, especially the kind that does not arise from regret.

Therefore, if both the wrong choice and the absence of one are insufficient, man is compelled to choose wisely, to make the choice that removes him from the sight of misery. Sound judgment becomes essential in reaching the sublime fascination that a right choice can bring, especially in realms dense with emotion, like love. Not everyone deserves your attention, and very few truly earn it. Misplaced investment leads to spiritual bankruptcy, a crushing debt in the currency of torment. So it is wise to remain cold until others show warmth, for if you burn too early, and for the wrong person, all that energy will be spent scorching your own mind.

Yet this does not mean that everything ends here, that with the ashes of moral suffering, the passion for living must also be extinguished. On the contrary, what remains may serve as fertile compost from which a new self may rise—stronger, grander, more commanding. In life, we owe more to those who did not want us than to those who did. In love and in friendship alike, it is the partings that dictate the most valuable lessons. Those to whom life has written only goodness have little to teach, little to recount.

Few things in this world are certain, but if you see someone who has fallen, suffered, and been reborn, more than once, then you are surely looking at a character forged in resilience, a formidable strength shaped by endurance. No one gets anywhere by being meek, for shyness erodes the path that steers away from desolation.

Thus, in choice lies an ambulatory way of being—a life that traverses the most unexpected existential peaks, charging toward an archetype of beauty, and rejoicing in a life sheltered within the realm of reward. And all it takes to be enveloped in this quiet fulfillment is one thing: power. The power to decide. The power to accept. And, perhaps most importantly, the power to go on.

It is a universal recipe—for every flavor of existence. And every human being is capable of preparing it, whether in the moment of first becoming or in the hour of final stillness. A subtle, pleasing, enchanting taste. Life provides the ingredients; it is man who must bring the strength to mix them. Without that strength, he spills them into the void.

So, if life composes an ode to power, of that power dense with consistency and the weight of acceptance, what, then, might it say about intelligence? Is intelligence a curse, a counterweight, or a formal identity? Or perhaps all of these, and more?

There is no remedy on earth for stupidity, only incentives to make it more conformist and more ambulatory. This, in essence, is the supreme trait of indifference toward the incurable, for the fool does not despise foolishness, but rather amplifies it, making it more virulent and contagious.

If we begin from the premise that the world is a realm of absurdity, then perhaps we can assert that intelligence is an exile, and stupidity a homeland. But why would that be? Perhaps because civilization has discredited sincere tears and glorified false smiles. Because people have unlearned how to be emotionally intelligent and now devour feelings suspected of duplicity. The essential difference lies in the fact that stupidity dwells natively and migrates through imitation, while intelligence dwells unnaturally and migrates through truth. Were it not so, society would no longer be the court jester of a world in decline, steeped in mediocrity. And it is somewhat inaccurate to say that stupidity has destroyed the world; it has not ruined anything. It has instead built a true marvel of nonsense.

Every societal inanity legally carries a depletion of significance, pinned into the eyes of all as a detour from misalignment. Of course, it's hardly admirable to align oneself with absurdity in submission to irrelevance, but it is what it is: a reality counterfeited by the banality of ideas discharged from the foundational condition of progress—ascension. Through stupidity, one ascends only into depth.

Moreover, intelligence is relative, it refers to something or someone, imbued with a volatile quality that evaporates easily in the overflow of the masses. Stupidity, on the other hand, is general, communal in collectivity, and it flows fluently through the masses, not to drown the individual in nonexistence, but to fill the emptiness with uniformity. An inept society is to an intelligent man what water is to a scorpion: the arachnid can survive underwater for two days, but it doesn't know how to swim.

Why is intelligence relative? Because it is measured through comparison. The first intelligent human was the one who discovered fire, an act that elevated his value. But can someone who lights something on fire today still be called smart? Of course not.

In their time, those considered intelligent were the ones who knew how to tell time, tie a knot, read, write, or possess general knowledge. As the years passed, it became those who could speak foreign languages, use technology, or complete formal education. So, when something clever becomes banal, people shift their perception of intelligence.

Decades ago, someone with a university degree was a rarity; maybe one or two people in an entire rural community. Now they're everywhere. Can we still affirm that intellectual quality is necessary to complete higher studies? That depends on each person's judgment.

Stupidity is an aesthetic paradox, it reveals a similar discrepancy. The Neanderthal who drowned from gluttony was a fool, just like the modern man who dies from an overdose. Where there is addiction, there is a gap, a rupture in the alignment between impulse and voluntary control. It's a stimulant, beneficial or harmful, that liberates one from the weight of perceiving the authentic world with clarity. The creation of addiction stems from the human need to live less complicatedly than lucidity demands. Whether it becomes destructive or life-enhancing depends on intelligence.

But a truly intelligent person is visible in the showcase of time—a distinct being honored with a title that inscribes them into the chronicle of their era. One who does everything possible to reveal human potential. Without such figures, progress wouldn't translate into realization. Nothing would solidify the awakening to meaning, because all development begins with the stillness of thought.

Hence, the questions arise: Has today's society advanced so far that intelligence has become common? Or has the bar been lowered so much that mediocrity has infiltrated excellence? Is someone with advanced studies truly superior, or simply mediocre? If things favor stupidity, if banality becomes the norm, then society has already released the scent of imminent and certain disaster into the air; a catastrophe summoned by the shrill whisper of incompetence.

To function well, to thrive in peace, a society needs the continual elevation of intelligence standards, so that human potential is not only tested but also materialized. Otherwise, not only are intellectual resources wasted, but reserves are also depleted, eventually exhausting the healthy rhythm of structure and organization.

Some might say that the dictatorship of mediocrity is installed through the majority of the ignorant masses, but that would be false, because such a majority has always existed. The intelligent have never gathered in numbers; they have only laid foundations. And even if we assume, just assume, that we now live in an age where stupidity is cheered as excellence, what is truly different?

Who still remembers the world in which ignorance was thought to be the root of stupidity? Is that belief still relevant, when everyone is now connected to a global web of information? Yes, everything has become too common and too accessible, which, in theory, isn't necessarily bad, but in practice, it has allowed the incompetent to ascend into high ranks. The real mistake, and the actual reason behind this decline, is that no measures have ever been devised to preserve intellectual superiority. Thus, the intelligent find themselves in a world where their skills and knowledge have been flattened into the nomenclature of banality.

So, in this condition, is intelligence merely asymptomatic, in a coma, or already dead? Why does life now breathe through an essence produced in the mold of mediocrity? It seems only mediocre people live according to life's current recommendation. For the rest, intelligence becomes a burden, a reversal of existence, where every step beyond the banal leads naturally to some obstruction, a resistance to the expansion of one's lived grace.

The intelligent can endure life only by imitating the ignorant. The reason is rather simple: the abundance of irrelevance dominates the structure of society, and denying it through utility-based criticism offers but one outcome—self-exile from nonsense. If someone perceives a widely embraced activity as foolish, they are left with two choices: detach from others, or pretend to care, for the sake of social camouflage.

For instance, one might find a match, a concert, a festival, or any such event, void of significance, which amplifies their sense of alienation. And since society is governed by the ungoverned momentum of stupidity, the intelligent are left with one path: to revise their behavior.

The stubbornness to display superiority ends up hiding it within the common inferiority, far from the unexpressed splendor of the masses—because people only honor their own arrogant posture of being remarkably ordinary. A revolt against the lack of exceptional qualities will never disturb the balance of mediocrity, the comfortable harmony of insignificance. That is why, in the spirit of involution, the intelligent one who began a rebellion of meaning ends up wrapped in incoherence. In this world, living at the normal temperature of intellectuality chills social relationships, while others, those less endowed, warm themselves by the fire of the ordinary, where life can only survive in the fever of nonsense.

In conclusion, if intelligence no longer grants social superiority through higher education, and cannot conform to the masses either, then what is its clinical status today? Is it still useful to be intelligent in modern times? Yes, but only exceptionally so. A strong critical analysis of every "flavor" of life deceives the deformity of living. All of them—love, freedom, happiness, success, faith, money, even time—resonate dissonantly when subjected to thinking. And yet, through thinking, even discord can be tuned into something agreeable.

Take money, for example—the most complex social equation—which heavily depends on a person's intellectual capacity to stop perpetuating existential crises. That alone shakes the tension rooted in escaping from suffering. There are more important things in life than money; competence is one of them. An incompetent person with financial power self-destructs, thoroughly and consistently, through a way of living that almost never suits them. Though abnormally privileged by wealth, they feel it is never enough, and thus end up in a fog of mental insufficiency that prevents them from fully experiencing happiness.

That intelligence isn't required to acquire wealth is true, but believing that success sustains itself intuitively or effortlessly is a lie. The true illusion of living apart from the obsession with making everything ugly merges two distant elements as a goal: one is reason, and the other temptation. Without thought, temptation punishes life; without temptation, thought does not educate it. In both cases, ugliness becomes a habit. Especially when, coupled with partial self-perception, the ugly becomes even more hideous through the exaggerated tendency to romanticize one's own underappreciated mistakes.

If in the material world subjectivism is a circumstantial reality—where each person cherishes a certain good more than another, and loss is perceived in accordance with individual understanding—things stand quite differently in the realm of emotion. In the domain of human relationships, objective intelligence becomes a decisive factor in merging initiation with permanence, because inflexible subjectivity inhibits repetition. More simply put, humans do not enjoy excessive constancy; except, perhaps, when aiming to serve an ideal.

A fitting example can be found in money. When an individual uses it in his own world, for personal interest, its influence obeys his subjective criteria and preferences. The consequences affect him alone, which confers a certain power over vulnerability to external dramas. Of course, the story changes entirely when the influence of money circulates in someone else's proximity; the power dynamics shift, and vulnerability to tragedy increases. If intelligence doesn't dance objectively, then others' steps fall out of sync. Money buys friendship, sells humanity, indebts envy, and redeems love.

Therefore, the universal circulation of thoughts, those that faithfully and unabridged reflect reality, offers a profound alternative to the craft of existing in superficiality. This aims to refine imperfections forged through the futile vocation of wandering in absurdity.

Far from the decay imposed by disregarding the laws of society stands only the one for whom money destroys what man does not honor—namely, what cannot be replaced: naivety. For if there is a science of cleverness, it surely contains an anecdote of the art of being naive. No one expresses a fall in reputation more than the gullible. A "reputation" is established only by those whose sharp minds sidestep any opportunity to be silently and unexpectedly deceived by their trust in others.

Unlike the fool, whose lack of trust arises naturally from aversion and shallow judgment, the naive person doesn't display a lack of intelligence but rather betrays a purity of innocence. Inner cleanliness is a virtue of the wise, but not so insoluble as to remain untouched by the grime typical of social living. It is the feeling that stains, not the act itself. A relationship may be tainted by betrayal of trust, but it cannot be sullied by the failure of a sincere act. In other words, one feels a betrayal deeply, no matter how small, but can endure a genuine failure with far greater ease.

Ultimately, for a person, disappointment caused by a small matter born of naivety weighs heavier than one brought on by grandiose foolishness. For instance, a friend is less likely to forgive another for revealing a secret, even an insignificant one, because that signals a void of trust that ends the notion of relying on him. Yet, the same friend may tolerate the destruction of personal belongings caused by stupidity. Thus, we discover something more precious than money: being stripped of one's naivety.

Nonetheless, naivety must be eradicated, especially in higher social hierarchies—but not only there. It should be purged even from one's close circles, from among friends and family.

Otherwise, no matter how intelligent a person is, if they are credulous toward their peers, they will face a deep and lasting impact from disappointment, particularly the kind that stems from human relationships. Therefore, intelligence requires objectivity when it comes to the potential consequences of interpersonal bonds.

This is especially vital for those in top positions rather than for those on society's common plateau, because social equilibrium is maintained by invisible, non-analytical mechanisms. In power structures, naivety becomes a structural weakness, one that is quickly exploited to gain one-sided advantages, discrediting the struggle for significance. Even religious reasoning can extrapolate the essence of caution. When you're down, God sends people to lift you. When you're up, the devil sends people to pull you down. That explains why, in the depths, it's wise to embrace any offered help, and at the peak, it's smart to carefully select every form of support.

If people were asked what the cruelest form of betrayal is, most would probably say: "When a friend stabs you in the back." Very few, however, would admit that betrayal by one's own mind is the perfect crime—one without witnesses. Why? Because that's where all hope, ambition, ideas, initiative, dreams, desires, and will are murdered. Yes, it hurts deeply when a friend sells you out in an instant, but why doesn't it hurt just as much when, for years, the mind indebts a person through procrastination, lack of confidence, hesitation, or fear?

It is not the violent sufferings of external betrayals that lead to defeat in life's battle, but rather the quiet betrayals of inner assent that bring forth a treaty of surrender. The entire explanation of this phenomenon stems from negation, from the fact that the mind is wired to halt denial through acceptance. If it weren't so, it would remain trapped in an infinite loop—for logically, one cannot end a denial by another denial, as that too would have to be refuted, and so on, endlessly. The only alternative to break the loop is through indifference, by ceasing to care about the subject, but in doing so, the problem is no longer solved, merely postponed outside the scope of concern.

So, when a person encounters difficulty, an impasse, or external hardship, the mind's first response is a compilation of suffering, which persists until the moment of calm, when the pain is assimilated into consciousness and no longer causes disruption. Acceptance is nothing more than a highly ingenious method of oppressing complexity into simplicity. Ultimately, it is ideal for things to unfold this way to prevent perpetuation and aggravation. Moreover, the individual is left with a valuable experience born of hardship, one that can also be seen as a karmic stumbling block, hindering the illusion that everything is owed to them.

Of course, things are not at all the same when battles arise as a result of inner turmoil, when suffering is triggered by a departure from the autonomous law of inner calm. Any pain, real or illusory, that originates internally rather than from external stimuli is also addressed by the brain through an automatic mechanism, but the means of resolution differ greatly from the previous case.

If the mind creates suffering, it cannot also produce rational acceptance, doing so would be nonsensical, a contradiction, a form of existential self-denial bordering on madness. When such an inner impediment arises, the brain signals the individual that help is needed, that external action is required to restore calm. It declares its helplessness through a tender melancholy.

What happens, and this is the most important aspect to understand, if the person does not respond to this call for support? Firstly, in such a case, ignoring is no longer an option; it becomes an aggravating lie and, as such, a response to be entirely dismissed. It's quite simple, like the principle: "live by the sword, die by the sword."

The second alternative, and by far the most common, is still rooted in acceptance, halting the cycle of denial through approval, but with a crucial difference: it no longer emerges from lucid awareness, as with conscious suffering. Rather, the mind generates a delusion of acceptance.

A person unable to maintain a relationship begins to be consumed by positive thoughts about solitude. Another, who lives in deep poverty, begins to believe that wealth brings trouble. A socially failed individual assumes that all successful people are privileged and corrupt. An uneducated person sees the educated in an unfavorable light. And the examples go on.

All these are nothing more than hallucinations produced by the brain to cope with internal suffering, which is generally stirred by deficiency. It's a brilliantly designed defensive mechanism for enduring life, but unfortunately, and herein lies the tragedy, it also becomes the silent catastrophe of existential surrender.

You endure in order to live, but you do not live in order to endure. Put more clearly, man no longer exists to conquer challenges; instead, his life is consumed by accepting that they are not necessary.

From this, one can deduce, regrettably, the path toward the

debasement and shattering of one's obsessions with leasing out reserves of limited time, because everything that has been lost in life was, beforehand, a victim of the demagogic threat of one's own thinking in the face of the moment. Suddenly, every failure criticizes the individual's inability to seize the moment, confirmed by the unconscious act of paying tribute to a counterproductive mind, after which, through an analysis of the outcome, it confers upon the failed person the status of an existential ghost; more plainly put, someone who has stripped their spirit of freedom by forcing it into delusion.

This leads us to a conclusion, not at all hasty, that inner betrayals are what cause the defeat of initiative and bring about a reconciliation with resignation, and which, quite credibly, represent the greatest enemy sabotaging one's mission to reveal the true person they could become. No one is truly undone by obvious external losses; all are destroyed by the frenzied inner illusion.

How could one logically attack a failure that has taken root inside them? Only through delusion. Many complain about their social situation, environment, parents, luck, anything external, when trying to justify a life lived in the shadows of misfortune. In his arrogance, man would rise and blame even the gods for the barrenness of his life, but he would not bow toward himself—thus blocking the path that leads in the right direction, the one that reveals the true reason for a dry and unsubstantial life—one of completely hollow experience.

This is why psychologists speak with such emphasis about self-awareness, a persistent talent that tirelessly grinds down and cleans away the daily routine of merging into sedentariness and conformism. The brain is remarkably cunning, capable of creating countless traps and tricks that capture the individual in a haze of orientational dizziness, seducing him into the ordinary comfort of stagnation. Its primary goal is survival, not to toil for the external prosperity of the human being. That is how it was architected, how it evolved over time, and this is precisely why progress breathes an extraordinary air: the atmosphere born from an inspiration of self-awareness.

No one truly knows the limit of thought, if such a limit exists, but what is certain is that we do know the mechanisms that block it. And that is vital to be aware of. Where one might arrive if released from the constraint of thought is unknown, but the possibilities are infinite, not merely metaphorically, but tangibly so. When the word *"infinity"* is invoked, the mind instinctively turns to the Universe, yet even its boundlessness remains speculative. Even infinity has its boundary: chaos. In certain simulations of complex systems, an infinite number of variables can still yield a finite result.

Yet the brain is not a chaotic blueprint—it is a dynamic enigma. For those who are conscious and wise enough to actualize it, the mind becomes a key unlocking an exceptional world, full of marvels in the making. For the rest, those immersed in the delusion of acceptance, it is a lock that traps them in astounding stagnation. If they do not fall into bitter unhappiness, they fall into the sin of judging life unjustly; with reproach and disgrace. And this, too, is a pathway to the threshold of what might be called "life dysmorphia"—that state where all of life's flavors are met only with displeasure, ugliness, and disgust.

Life grants nothing; it seizes everything. It does not even give us "lemons", for when bitterness arrives, it is only because sweetness has been taken away. Only man is mandated in this world to give, and in return for this service, he receives meaning.

Being a thinking animal, man projects every opinion he forms about his world as a supposition, a gesture meant to glorify his attempts to practice a spiritual vocation. The initial emergence of reasoning leads to a conclusion, good or bad, that the mind, for a moment, escapes the prolonged possibility of hatred, simply by admitting something to be real, true, in communion with nature. For hatred does not arise from spirit, but from emotion, and emotions are subjective. Therefore, hatred does not exist from the start; it appears only at the end, as the consequence of emotional damage incurred during the logical chain leading to deduction.

If someone assumes they do not like something or someone, they are unlikely to reach the harsh moment of aversion, they will instead shift their course of action based on a new supposition, this time a favorable one. Thus, primary judgment cannot begin with disdain, much less can it despise something concrete simply for existing; such a stance would be an unfounded complex. Why hate the wolf for hunting sheep? That is its nature.

And yet, why do some people turn hatred into an immediate cause? Because, beyond reason, humanity possesses a unique trait: the capacity for imagination, the ability to honor the nonexistent at the expense of the perceptible. In some instances, this can be harmful; in others, fruitful. It becomes a destructive trait when it interferes with primary judgment, when a supposition no longer synthesizes truth but instead absorbs the barren illusion of a mirage forged in the desert of the mind. In this way, a premise mutates into a prejudice.

Sure, in exceptional ambiguity, there are times when a prejudice proves to be correct, but that merely reinforces the exception. In principle, almost any thought adopted beforehand is inherently flawed, because it is grounded in inexperience, in untested assumptions, in ignorance. If it turns out to be accurate, it can only be attributed to an exceptional intuition or a coincidental convergence of outcomes, a rare mathematical chance.

If the prejudice turns out to be false, it may be unpleasant, but it is normal. Normal, because it was never detached from illusion, untruth, or ignorance. Whoever expects precision in their analysis without having measured reality is caught in a delirium of hope. Sadly, the number of those who form faulty prejudices is vast, and rather than guiding them from confusion to clarity, these ideas drag them from confusion to disillusionment.

All people form prejudices in resistance to the vitality of the unknown. The fact that an unknown thing imposes itself forcefully in the mind is revealed in the dimension of nothingness, because paradoxically, the absence of information occupies more mental space, through its limitless confusion, than a compressed enigma does when sealed into prejudice.

Prejudice, by its nature, is the brain's attempt to ease the burden of the unknown through the comforting weight of error.

Well, in the end, all that remains for such individuals is to realize they are not meant for a spiritual vocation. In this particular case, too many thoughts do not resolve the issue, they compound it into a tangled complexity. The reason is simple: as the number of thoughts increases, so does the number of unknowns, and naturally, everything turns into a great obsessive confusion. If excessive thinking is not nourished by reality but thrives in illusion, it becomes an idealistic affliction. Infection with this reflex poisons one's way of living; life is consumed in the spirit of multiplying emptiness, that void found in the heart of a dead end, where the only apparent exit seems to lie in thoughts gone awry—a delirium of searching for something that exists in nowhere.

The overproduction of thought is an obsession with ugliness born at the departure of perfection, for not everything in this world aspires to a grand ideal. Even man is a being contracted to imperfection. This is easy to see: before the mirror, perfection resigns. Either he becomes tormented and obsessed by minor flaws, developing a kind of body dysmorphia, or he fails to notice them altogether, falling into a form of self-adoration. In both scenarios, perfection is the premise, and ugliness the arrival.

The same applies to all elements composing a human life. One wrestles with too many thoughts until, in effect, they lose the battle with a serene existence and become overwhelmed by the aesthetics of distortion. Every flavor of life is vulnerable to preconception, overthinking, brooding, or judgment, and when people intensify the workings of the mind in pursuit of perfection, none escape the contagion of "life dysmorphia." In the end, what remains is the bitter conclusion that fantasy, when joined with falsehood, ignorance, or inexperience, concocts a distasteful mixture of life's flavor, one that proves damaging to many. Even disagreeable, for distortion is, in essence, the right not to be suitable.

In contrast with the grinding, harmful fantasy, the one that shames existence through the human capacity to forge new, corrosive representations, dangerously leaning toward the denial of spiritual dignity, stands the other noble invention: imagination. This is the virtue that constitutes the absolute perfection of idea factories. Without imagination, humanity would have been left wide open inside a prison devoid of variety. Everything would conform to a replica of the primordial original, to a creation illuminating only its belonging to the void—a kind of absurdity where nothing could stand apart from the dull fulfillment of being.

Every flicker of imaginative thought leads man into an exile of uniqueness, far from the homeland of the trivial, where he is welcomed by the decency of being a distinguished compatriot of the exceptional. In truth, the ordinary scorches wherever imagination fails to cast its gaze, especially in that singular situation when "there" becomes "everywhere." Indeed, the absence of fantasy is visible in all things and in every place, from the most tangible object to the most abstract notion. Money, happiness, success, even love—all fall under the spell of the imagined. Because banality signs in everything, yet when one says "the most banal thing," the reference is to sex devoid of imagination.

From the earthworm to the king, from the moth to the scholar, mating fits neatly into biology when fantasy fails to seep into the moment of union, proving the essential role of conception in the individuation of love. Speechless creatures do not differ in their joining; they lack the vibration of comprehension. But man is gifted with a thinking temperament that qualifies him for a state of powerful exaltation, but only when imagination lifts him above animal instinct.

Hence, purely and incisively, cynically and truthfully, it is declared: only those who possess a rare mind can brazenly claim disqualification from the animal kingdom—not biologically, but imperceptibly, spiritually.

Had imagination never existed, humanity would be unworthy

of observation, passionless, absent from wonder entirely. The world and the cosmos would be barren lands, failures in the uniformity of emptiness. The conceptual ability inspired by imagination is of divine essence, and every creation remains loyal to the initial dream of its founder. And if it does not, then life slowly devolves into a superficial longing to legitimize the farce of inertia.

Imagination drives and shifts the frequency by which the outer world is analyzed, transforming our perception of reality into a realm of fiction—where ideas are conceived, only to escape later and reshape the real world.

Indeed, the transposition of an idea from fantasy into truth is only possible through the will of the one who harbors it within the machinery of thought, namely, the human being, who is simultaneously the initiator, the attendant, and the finisher. There are two paths to becoming an inventor: to feel distant from the present, and to feel the stretch of the future. More clearly put, imagination carries the individual into a realm of reverie, from which they retrieve conceptions once far removed from the objective world, nestled near the unreality that lay adrift in the horizon of time. Every visionary crosses abstract thresholds and bypasses tangible limits, but only if they rise above passivity. Perhaps the one who possesses the gift of imagination and does not bring it to life represents the most wasted talent of the age.

Those who are neglectful should no longer await fulfillment, it always arrives too late for those who postpone. And the lazy should no longer hope for success—it never embraces the idle. Let them cry into the irrelevance of their own making until the impurity within becomes a trait, like in a hallucination, and the time they squandered carries the ache of the unachieved into the shallow depths of regret, until suffering settles into their consciousness like ash after fire.

Yes, otherwise the person who surpasses their own existence in imagination but never brings it into being remains lost in an illusory void, from which they draw all the sap of their unhappiness; born of unfulfillment. And the only path to salvation lies in the ambition to let go. Sometimes, one must be brave enough to be ambitious in relinquishment. It is not desirable, but it is healthy—because he who possesses a remarkable mind and fails to employ it meaningfully will be tormented until not even the will to breathe remains in him. A total resignation, cloaked in silence.

The absurdity of fantasy becomes most apparent when imagination begins to relate to the non-existent, things that cannot be materialized, and to falsehoods. Imagination stoops low when it fabricates a lie, and the individual who masters the art of deception in the name of self-interest becomes a veiled social threat: immoral yet richly imaginative.

Yet, beyond its negative aberrations, imagination remains the most complete miracle of human existence. Without it, humanity would have nothing to be admired for, no purpose, no hope, no ideals, only a dull, animalistic, miserable being: ugly, inert, and bleak. Man would still climb trees for fruit if someone hadn't once imagined a ladder. He would still dwell in caves if architecture had never been conceived. He would be a stranger to joy if entertainment, sport, and culture had not emerged. He would love like a mountain loves its rock, had there been no romantic fantasy. He would have believed in the void had religion not granted him spiritual essence. He would have sold existential numbness had the economy not intervened. He would have spoken through gestures if words had not acquired meaning. He would have listened to the silence of the ages, were it not for the pouring forth of music.

Everything that exists in this structured world, our society, is the consequence of imagination's spirit, which drew from invented nonexistence those morsels of truth that added value to actual life.

Of course, not everything born of imagination holds the same weight of importance or necessity for human existence. Some things are trivial, mere comforts of preoccupation, while others become inseparable from the very sense of being. A toy is the product of an idea, one for which some dedicate their entire lives. That doesn't necessarily make it vital, nor that life couldn't go on without it, perhaps with a replacement, but it still adds a faint hue to the environment. Things carry different meanings; they don't have to be equally useful or complex to be meaningful. Even something as simple as a coat becomes critical in a storm, still, a result of imagination's depths.

Imagination is the genius of all. It is remarkably gracious with creation, but not equally so with sublime meaning. Because, without exaggeration, many human inventions have taken the form of banality. At times, reflecting on tangible reality, one could reach the bleak conclusion that imagination has also been a virulent force, spreading disease across the world. And you might rightly wonder: would society still suffer from so much poor taste if fantasy hadn't existed?

Still, things seem to balance, albeit superficially, its brighter side being more obvious. But one cannot help but imagine what the world would have looked like had imagination, the seed of creation, been cleansed of its harmful traits. After all, a sword and a pen, a cannon and a violin, a trap and a cure, all are products of imagination. The Creator must have had immense trust in mankind to endow it with such monumental power to conceive, capable of shaping both the elegance of art and the machinery of war.

Art is the paradisiacal smile that decisively delivers a final, direct, and resounding verdict on humanity: it had no God without the aesthetics it birthed. Without art, the world would have lacked substance, been content with deficiency and deformity, trapped in a dramatic contact with the impossibility of admiration. Generally, it would have found its inspiration in a pathological impulse toward erasure. For the artist brings with them the divine talent of working eloquently in a world void of expressiveness. And from the chronological weave, an idea can be tailored that places the human in an entirely unused state within a suggestive reality, because when something beautiful and accomplished is felt, the entire geometry of existence leans toward creation.

In truth, if beauty is not stimulated and deformity is encouraged, the entire concept of being unfolds in total abandonment of creation, close to a surrender of the pride that once maintained contact with reality—into a grand sentiment of dullness. It's not merely about tangible creation, what can be seen or touched, it is even more important to note that art shapes the human perception and intensifies one's experience of living, making one more receptive to the seduction of life. The influence of beauty enhances appreciation for love, freedom, happiness, and, as a result, it generates pleasant feelings and fosters will. This is why music is a symbol of willing stimuli, which passionately ease the frenzied pressure of time. Music is the deepened dream within unsleep. Every form of art is a great enemy of deformity and a true friend of disposition.

Usually, that disposition is good, though rarely, it may be bad, but the standing statement remains: Humanity was a lost herd in nothingness without art.

Another important point to mention is that the artist is the fortunate resolution of time's unending tragedy. Why? Because they compress and extract, from an infinity of possibilities, within a single moment of creation, a finite array of selections. This is what renders our world marked by absolute uniqueness in the unfolding of time.

If parallel universes were to exist, they would be fundamentally different along the chronological axis, in expression, in appearance, in representation, for what has come into being here exists as emptiness there; and vice versa. A philosopher who has written a book, composed of a multitude of words, ordered in a mathematically near-infinite way, influenced by countless immeasurable factors, holds the assurance that their work could only be replicated at the very end of eternity. For time to subject an artist's creation to resemblance, to erase it from uniqueness, it must first reach completion—infinity itself. Only then, when all possible combinations have been exhausted, will a perfect replica emerge.

Yet, an act of refinement must occur in the solution of creation. Not every creative act carries the same concentration of existential significance, nor does each bear the weight of being reproducible only in eternity.

Invention, for instance, does not aspire to the reverence of the incalculable. If humanity were to start over from zero a thousand times, then in each instance, at some point along its timeline, the lightbulb would be invented. If there are advanced extraterrestrial civilizations, they too have undoubtedly discovered artificial light. An invention is merely the detection of how to surpass a limitation; nothing more complex. But art—art is something else entirely. It is the careful sorting of methods meant to briefly express the symbolism of the infinite.

And human life itself is a selection of deliberate or chaotic events, slowly revealed from the unseen participation of the infinite in the world, so that living becomes a spectacular work of styling the possibilities derived from the multifaceted offerings of reality. Humanity is shaped against the current of time, it inhales a general imperfection drawn from the unchangeable past, and it subsists through the particular intensity of what is possible, for as long as the unlimited endures, the incomplete remains adaptable. Only at the end will everything be perfected and unchangeable. Until then, humanity is condemned to survive among the inadequate and to thrive by adapting imagination to reality.

In the end, aesthetic perception is what beautifies an individual's experience. Sometimes, the bitterness fades when one consumes what others have prepared. Other times, one must craft their own sweet substance, flavored by the delight of fantasy. And not everything must be purely theoretical, fully lucid, or absolutely true. Sometimes, it's better not to ask why 2 + 2 equals 5, but to find something beautiful in that extra one. If everything were bound by precision, nothing would hold charm in a human life; everything would be an eternal reproach of the immutable. It is the error, and the pursuit of improvement, that give existence its special flavor—infusing it with intent. The only question that truly extricate life is: *"Why is the answer always continuity?"* The grace of living is a privilege reserved for those who do not stop, for those whose mediocrity in stagnation does not outweigh their admiration for overcoming, or worse, does not submit to it.

It is only for those who endure when placing a foot beyond the threshold of difficulty. And that step comes as a reflex of conscience, a subtle call urging the individual to summon persistence and courage to move the stillness. If everyone were to remain where they are, humanity would crowd itself into a torturous space alien to progress, anesthetized by the last contemplation of creation, unstable in its dreaming, and no longer serving itself, but rather falling back into the animal kingdom.

The mark of an evolving human lies in not presenting himself as resigned, but in acknowledging defeat, for there is a difference between being lost and being a loser. The one who still finds pleasure in contemplating victory is the defeated; the other has made peace with loss. Nature cascades into decay, decay into extermination, and extermination into death. Life is a struggle because annihilation is not an option—it is merely an example of the end. Hence the sincere deduction, born of a loyal paradise: to live is to battle, nothing endures without the presence of struggle. In nature, one observes beauty, the mirror of a universal wonder, the true miracle of life, the essence of cherishing the dream made real, and above all, a reverence is owed to all triumphs.

For we marvel at the spectacle of a volcano, yet it burned everything around it to exist;

A river flows with soothing grace, but only after it carved the mountain apart;

A tree gives luscious fruit, yet it smothers the plants beneath it;

A swamp sustains rich biodiversity, yet it drowned all that stood before it;

A mushroom grows only by consuming decay;

A tiger survives by feeding on other being;

And every colony implies, somewhere in its foundation, an act of annihilation.

Everything that exists is born of a struggle to destroy—the vanquished disappears, while the victorious rises with effort. Yet within the grand architecture of this world, within the horizon of this noble planet, in the glass case bounded by sky and earth, there is a special case of nature, one whose existence is consumed at the temperature of abstraction, breathing vapors of the unknown and swallowing loss like fluid. One for whom life becomes a prescription for a journey through time, and the nearness of the end brings about a state of pale acceptance. That being is none other than man.

He is the only animal that voluntarily traverses the detours of life: at times strong or weak, cultured or unknowing, accomplished or failed, creator or futile, victorious or broken, sociable or reclusive, humble or arrogant—and the list goes on. And the choice is made by answering the existential conflict at the core: Do you fight in order to be, or do you exist in order to fight? You either go through the ordeal to become someone, or remain someone who endures the ordeal. This is the attestation upon which destiny is pronounced. Life gives the verdict, and through intentional resistance, man amends the ordinary and the irrelevant.

If you analyze humanity as a whole, as a collective, you adapt it to tragedy; but if you observe it in detail, in individuality, you reconcile it with greatness. It is spectacular to witness certain personal achievements, and bitterly disheartening to examine society. All these gaps and completions, these shifts and compensations, are entirely due to the circulation of thought, which steps unpredictably, deformed or precise, clear or obscure, nostalgic or visionary, along the trail of time.

Imagination, reason, and memory have all agreed to disregard the rules of the Universe—the existential game—because, unlike other living beings that dwell in harmony with nature, man has rightfully considered himself a founding, ungovernable entity. The only subjugation he participates in is that of betrayal; self-betrayal. And as a reversal of the medal for that mental distinction, unavailable to other species, man becomes the only creation of nature that defeats itself in the most disgraceful way: through a lack of respect and honor. No other species allows itself to deny its own being or its own life; all are fixed in their living non-being. Marching through the fluidity of thought quenches the thirst for the unknown but floods the rejection of one's own character, and standing still in the dryness of rigid convictions dries up even the last desire for ascension. No matter what a person reveals in their life, if they have lost themselves, they can no longer find a reason to exist. Perhaps only the divine could still help. No one can hide you from death, but it is God who reveals you for life.

Moreover, if you stop to consider that man is the only being attempting to draw support from the Creator through the very act of seeking connection, then the multipolarity of reason begins to oscillate with a simplified intensity toward a singular form of deduction; that this phenomenon too might be a gift born of imagination. And if this hypothesis holds true, then it affirms divine intervention in the real world, extrapolated through fantasy itself.

Since the world is saturated with manifestations of imagination, embedded in every field, activity, or profession, why should faith alone be the exception, the only imagined construct that does not spill over into truth? In fact, those who negate the Creator by associating Him with imagination are unknowingly offering a positive testimony; for even through the frameworks of negation, imagination flows like a divine breeze through reality—remodeling, reordering—a chaos refined by reverie.

Indeed, the entire existential question is a pure enigma, complicated by two wildly unpredictable variables, imagination and chaos, that resist any formula intelligible to man. This leads to a singular resolution: these are values of creation itself.

Thus, imagination becomes more telling than rationalism in distinguishing man from beast. A purely rational being, devoid of imagination, shares more with the voiceless animals than someone whose thoughts are flavored by fantasy's freshness. Presumably, all people carry some measure of imagination, though it may often hide behind inconvenient losses in unreality. The ultimate unveiling of the self is the remnant of character that has endured the existential battles each person fights in the pursuit of a reputation as something more; something transcendent. The fear of being like the rest fuels this inner competition, a struggle with one's own thoughts that arises as a directive to awaken consciousness to a life aligned with purpose. And more than fear, it is the courage of self-transcendence that crowns one as a valiant warrior, triumphing over personal ruin.

For all other creatures, the battle against annihilation is fought outwardly, but for man, the war is internal—raging within the theater of the mind. Only he who gains mastery over his thoughts emerges victorious; for if the mind is not ruled, it will incite toward error. Then no flavor will spark anything joyous, pleasant, or beautiful, and life's savor will blend into an overwhelming bitterness of imagined injustice.

Yet all states born of emancipation from the burden of thought, even those pressed under the weight of negative temptations, are, by far, more revelatory than any other form of understanding. The condition is that man must accept honesty as the voice of self-education. If he can do this, he becomes a graduate of hope, not a candidate for failure by disfigurement. The flavors of life reflect on a savor prepared in definitive beauty, and the sequence of moments lived becomes a stream of steady experiences, free from the convulsions of life's dysmorphia. The recipe for living beautifully contains this one essential principle: self-respect.

10

The recipe of life

So, in the end, after all these contradictions, after every thought that generates a relative idea, after the plastic vision of shaping truth or falsehood, after the unfolding of the temptation to adore illusion or reality, after the betrayal or triumph of conscience, after the assertion before nature of imaginative secrecy—there comes, after a long confusion, a purifying, essential, and edifying question that seeks to clarify everything: What is the recipe for the "Flavor of Life"?

The answer is simple, and identical to the recipe itself: there is none. There is no other recipe for living than the universal one: to prepare a human being. The flavors of life unfold gracefully when people carry within themselves an intimate substance, of the purest human elegance, blending the valence of existence with the voluptuousness of living, without spilling external or internal impurities.

It is not so important for the individual to delve obsessively or exceptionally deep into the flavor they adore, as it is to gain the ability to sift through the disgust, even if only a small detail of a problem. In an abundance of wealth, in immense financial power, life can be destroyed in a single moment of misdirection, entirely and irreparably, and all that remains is the cruel feeling of being grateful for the end. A long period of coexistence in profound love, with passion and care, with attentiveness and joy, with endless conversations, can end in the contrast of a single sentence. Years of labor in pursuit of accomplishment can be ruined by the deviation of a single mistake. When a person listens to the tone of ugliness, music becomes a source of displeasure, of horror, of all that resonates with negativity—and they are left with nothing but to dance to the steps of deformity.

The "Life dysmorphia" does not arise from ignorance of a recipe for living, but from the structure of a conscience that ponders with thoughts extending beyond the scope of proper conception. This dysmorphic defect of perception has nothing in common with the correspondence to the demands of living; rather, it has allied itself with a prejudice formed outside the sphere of reasons for existence; it is a stubborn disturbance obsessed with imperfection. Surely, nothing is perfect, everything trembles with deficiencies, and the collapse of life stems from the obsession to fill absence with preconceived ideas, which do not complete the void, but contaminate it with concern.

Self-awareness is vital in order to avoid beginning a new life with the cursed power of scorning one's original existence— the fleeting one, enriched by the sympathy of pleasure, that inconvenient life that begs not to be avoided. It is the most basic plus that subtracts a minus of deformity in the act of living, for it diminishes, with manifold measure, the unpleasantness born from a reality distorted by the equation of hostility, until man begins to perceive a reality that leans toward favor. If he was not born with favor, then he has no choice but to gather it himself.

Of course, there may be other virtues, some drawn from faith, others from illusion, perhaps even from suffering, but in concrete terms, all people carry deficits of perception, flaws in fairness, or insufficiencies in knowledge. These are what define human nature as inherently enigmatic. From this arises a conclusion, by way of deduction: that humanity is sentenced to self-understanding. No one is entitled to hand over a recipe for life to another, let alone instruct someone in the path to self-discovery. Not because some wouldn't be capable or well-intentioned, but for the simple reason that each individual is immersed in their own mystery—one that can only be resolved through introspection, through the revelation that startles the ego. Does a donkey wait to be taught how to be a donkey? Then why should man expect others to prepare the recipe for how to be human? It is his mission, his calling, to understand what he is. If he is seduced by atypical diversions, by distorted forms, by countless trivialities, it will be difficult for him to penetrate the central axis of his autonomous expedition. The temptation to slide into a faded self-image lies at every step. And with every denouncement of despair, with every nightmare lulled into destruction, with every corruption-induced ruin, the individual sweeps away any possession that might compromise him in a broader degradation.

There can be no pouring of life's flavor into existence while impurities are constantly being spilled, for man is born immaculate, with an absolute purity—one that clothes him in a form susceptible even to the most subtle stain. When a lion is born, it is known a beast has arrived, eager to begin its life of killing. But when a human is born, he is marked by a known truth: innocence; which makes him vulnerable to the lure of deviation. His bondage in this life is tied to himself, to his own being, through the ideal condition of not becoming a captive to some irrelevant, aimless force that draws him into despair, but rather, of becoming a prisoner of perfected self-mastery.

In practical terms, life has a biological beginning, and countless ideological restarts, which forces a continual recalibration of the self. This process is essential, lest the person run on in confused and damaging loops, plagued by an unfit malfunction of consciousness. One can function, in full self-possession, only by learning to carry gratitude, whether joyous or painful, for that very act defies adversity. It dissolves the impulse to subsidize existence through vengeance, whether figurative or material. And this self-mastery cannot be planted by another; it is a state sown by one's own will in the cultivated soil of their mentality.

That is why the recipe for being human cannot be prepared by harvesting the fruit of others. It must be crafted in the place where others cannot tread—in the internal industry of one's own understanding. And to forge a skilled character, each person must process as much information as possible—good or bad—must absorb as much experience as they can—pleasant or painful—and must gather as many ingredients—sweet or sour—as life will offer.

In no book, no speech, no conversation, no situation, will anyone ever find a magic formula that transforms life into a splendid spectacle. One may find, at best, fragments, elements that, if consciously embraced, might help bring their personality closer to a state of revelation.

Perhaps the most sinister social deception of the modern age is the ambition to teach others how to live. Every human takes the final exam of being at the moment of departure from this world, at the judgment beyond, thus, no one is truly qualified to instruct others in the art of humanity, let alone dictate the proper direction of life. Not parents, not friends, not mentors, not idols, not even the accomplished—no one is truly capable of stating a valid way to live within the human condition. It remains the responsibility of each individual to soar toward the horizon of a precise unknown; knowledge is a floating with no destination, a gliding toward the rarefied edge of all things. Even a bird discovers with its own wings that the limit is the sky, never by relying on another's beak.

When a man confines himself to learning from others how to swim, he either remains on the shore or drowns. But when he distances himself from the depth of instruction and practices active repetition, he floats in self-overcoming. It is only then that the ability and will to cross the turbulence can rise to the surface. This is why no one and nothing can, by persuasion or chance, conceive a universal solution or procedure to transfer life's preparation from one person to another. The recipe of life is inseparable from self-knowledge.

This book, too, does not violate that rule; its aim is not to provide a formula for existence. It is sprinkled with ingredients, perhaps confusing or contradictory, with the intent that they be extracted and blended into the mixture of one's own thinking. Each person is entitled, without homogenization, to reason in harmony with their own universe. For naturally, such is life, with agreement and disagreement, contradiction and resonance, model and anti-model, clarity and entanglement, negation and affirmation. In essence, the human condition is saturated with duality, and it falls upon man to extract the essential elements in order to form the chemistry between himself and life.

The world changes more through the power of example and experience, and less through the weakness of education. Social transmission of skills and behaviors is limited to collective knowledge, while example and experience depend on individual diligence. Education forms a citizen who begins at an origin and reaches a destination, repeating daily the posture of that finalized character. In contrast, through transcendence and reason, through and by self-learning, emerges a person who begins anew each day—estranged from finality, a citizen of no end.

This does not mean that education is wrong, harmful, or useless; it simply indicates that it is a limited bubble of knowledge, representing a collection of aphorisms, theorems, and principles characterized by prior learning and dedicated to information extracted from celebrated reality; generally speaking. The problem of education lies in a temporal paradox: it reveals the past in an attempt to mask the future through the dissimulation of the present, leading to a persistent misalignment within the constancy of change.

If we account for the variable of progress, the certainty of transformation, then it becomes evident that the educated person, in their current standard, remains a repeater until they pass the threshold of adaptability. Thus, the one who emerges from the bubble of education with the intent to understand the vital phenomena of development reaches a powerful expression of the masterpiece forged through personal reflection. It is also important to acknowledge that without education, nothing is possible, it is essential to human evolution, as it synthesizes a vast trove of information that no one could gather alone. It is an indispensable ingredient in preparing a recipe for living. However, anyone wishing to transcend their limits must first participate in the sphere of shared knowledge, and when they begin to sense the boundaries of information forming around them, they must step beyond the collective sphere to trace a life path without limits.

But returning to the power of individuation, the world is transformed either when you change a fool, or when you change everyone. But the only one truly within reach is the "self." No other number of people changed between these two poles can bring about a general transformation, for after each person reformed, a mathematical expression still applies: several billion remain. This is why, in the spirit of social progress, it is far more effective for a person to offer themselves, willingly or unwittingly, as an example of success, and far less effective, perhaps entirely so, to attempt to teach others how to succeed. An example is imitated, while instruction is merely absorbed; through examples, many are gathered who desire change, while through lessons, many are gathered who merely know how to observe it.

Likewise, a great problem in this world stems from the indirect education of conformity, the ideology of approval, a notion that dissipates into society a general attitude of being too good, in the worst sense of the word. Disagreement is no longer contradicted, nor is risk, discomfort, delay, mistake, challenge, impulse, or any of the dual elements that conspire toward the condescension of disfigurement. There must always be bad in this world, so that good is unoccupied by irrelevance, and connivance finds an application. One must not confuse bad with evil, for failure in an exam may be bad, but it is not the end; revolt may be bad, yet it yields reform;

weeping may be bad, yet it spills a tear of empowerment. For good to thrive in visibility and substance, bad must exist in context—distinguished and contended with.

Thus, when all is erased through compliance, when contradiction is absent, when arguments go unchallenged, when all danger is praised through ignorance, and when everything is distributed by approval—nothing remains to be affirmed. Goodness becomes helpless and stagnant. The solution, as an ingredient in preparing a recipe for being human, must be blended with the inner substance that emits the vapor of effort, sustaining the flame that burns through inaccessibility to a smoke-free existence. Put differently, evil smolders unceasingly and smokes out human aspirations until, finally, a person chooses to ignite and reduce to ash all that clouds their life. And this pyromania—figuratively speaking, of course—cannot be kindled without a spark of internal ruthlessness and, likewise, a trace of external harshness.

In conclusion, the education of conformity imputes a reprovable deformity, one that drowns life in the occupation of absorbing nebulousness into its vision. The only light comes from grasping the symbiosis of good and evil.

Sure, there are also positive arguments, especially collective ones, particularly economic, for mechanical acceptance and formal submission to consensus. Yet individuality, and, why not, humanity itself, suffers over time. If something harmful becomes embedded in society, something that appears good on the surface but is rotten at its core, and people are not wicked enough to criticize it, destroy it, and humiliate it, then it will not vanish from the community. If they are sufficiently tolerant toward the evils in their own lives, whether by ignoring or failing to notice them, they will propagate that same attitude into their surroundings.

The "No" awakens contradiction, which rocks the cradle of reason. The "Yes" lulls denial, stirring the tide of conformity. Perhaps the only indisputable freedom is the freedom to question what is already known, to challenge it with a conception that grants a capacity for critical consciousness, without descending fully into the quarrel of ideological conflict. The world loses itself in the agreement of consistency, in the absence of categorical refusal of contradiction. And it is essential for man not to forget rejection, but also not to be seduced by absolute negation, for through conformity he omits the extreme lucidity of his human condition. He endures the comfort of non-judgment, a passivity that lures him into the raw hope of believing in universal innocence. The naive, usually, is merely an anonymous to refusal.

Therefore, no one can change their life, themselves, or the world, without the inspiration of disagreement, the harmony of contradiction, especially the ability to recognize evil, to identify it, and to combat it with a serious "No" spoken at the right moment. That "No" purifies the imprecision of change and brings forth a behavioral transformation born of self-awareness—of the inept reflex of uncritical approval, of comfortable, docile submission.

Rejection is a virtue of filtration when one prepares an existential recipe, for it separates harmful elements from the final product; from life's savor. And without this filter, an indispensable tool that helps man halt the impurities spilled by time into the blend of his experiences, he becomes susceptible to harmful.

Speaking of time, it is itself a dimensional fluid that submerges the conformist person into various traps of passivity, enveloping them in wastefulness. Thus, the awareness and refusal to fall into the sluggishness of duration is imperative for the one who fights for the value of the moment. Waiting and procrastination must be renounced as part of one's daily expenditure of energy. Waiting is a paradox of time: when you wait, time passes slowly but is consumed quickly. You know, when you set a vacation and keep thinking, "The day won't come soon enough," and then, after the holiday, you look back and say, "How fast the year has gone."

A similar thing happens during winter when many await the holidays with impatience, ignoring the days leading up to them, days they would fast-forward through if they could. Both waiting and postponing are mental states that poison the moment, for they trap the mind in a distant perspective. The result is that people waste their days dreaming of a future objective instead of valuing the present as they should. In the end, everyone will realize that the days flew by, and they won't know how.

Presumably, the best analgesic for the ailment of time is to be creative. If fun burns through time, creativity freezes it; it destroys the perception that the years have flown by because it leaves something behind—something measurable, something that testifies to time well spent. For those who believe it's too late to create, they should study cases of elderly individuals who triumphed after retirement, who began creating after 70 and became renowned artists. Waiting penetrates the vigor of hope, while procrastination becomes the chastity of laziness. Hope within laziness prolongs the true lie of acquired happiness. Not that one cannot be happy in laziness, but if it becomes organized, if it descends into pure inactivity, then all that remains is for the ban on pleasure to be lifted by the truth that man, as an agent of doing, is sometimes forced by circumstance to fail.

Practically, the lazy person is caught in a tension between submission and liberation: on one hand, submitted to resignation and liberated from pressure, and on the other, submitted to failure and liberated from will—one gentle, the other inhumane. If he sees only the acceptable half, born from the self-sabotage of contentment, he may continue to coexist within the characteristic style of complacency, he may encounter happiness, peace, and calm, for resignation and the absence of pressure combine to simulate a vision of tranquility. Yet it is a fate constrained by unilateral orientation, a decoration won by the game of losing, a theme from which to sketch blueprints of abandonment that, like a drug, demands raw devotion to the directive of passivity. A mere glance away, a conceptual contact with the ruthless side, may destroy the world of nullity that the lazy man has built, manipulated as he is by the revealing thought.

His existential indifference does not lie in total inactivity, but only in the external kind, the one that does not fulfill an observable intent. However, he is not necessarily intellectually inactive, as that belongs to another category—namely, the fool—a fact which complicates the lazy man's situation beyond the simplicity it suggests. Thus, thoughts do not necessarily avoid the direction of relaxation, and any revealing idea of truth may very well be encountered during the indulgent course of disinterest.

If not for the dread instilled by reason, all people would desire to be lazy—thus, judgment becomes the mask that suppresses inactivity. Who wouldn't wish to dwell in total indifference if not for the burden of conscience? It is precisely understanding that lifts man out of the paradise of ease and anchors him in the hell of tension; that strain born of the need to be someone, to do something, to work chaotically, to curse rest, to live beneath the pressure of outcome.

This does not imply that the lazy person lives estranged from the craft of comprehension; rather, he earns his existence by defaming understanding itself. He transforms it into a metric for stepping away from the mechanism required to endure engagement. It's a courteous concession to inconvenience, yet defiant toward productivity, within which indiscipline becomes an outcry against the vital bond with the ethics of labor.

Some might offer a counterpoint, suggesting that laziness fosters inventiveness because the lazy seek ways to avoid hard work. But truthfully, to frame laziness as a virtue is a blasphemy against the doctrine of the accomplished doer. It is not a virtue; it is a minor offering, a compressed burst of energy built up from prolonged inactivity. It cannot endure. If invention arises from it, if it happens that the lazy mind glimpses the horizon where effort has set and ease has risen, it merely suggests that, had this person persevered under steady labor, there might have emerged not just a clever trick, but a radiant emblem of genius—not merely a spark of cunning.

Therefore, the issue is not whether laziness is innate or acquired, whether it is a biological inclination or a learned posture. Either way, it is an existential career to which one commits in order to pursue no purpose at all. Put otherwise, it is a mode of living that nearly always relegates the person to insignificance.

For the inactive, there are two ways to be uncommitted: one is a form of laziness filled with peace and empty of tasks; the other, a laziness emptied of acceptance and filled with the dead weight of failure. It would not be offensive to call such a person a specialist in freedom, if only he were not tormented by his dependence on one singular thing: the squandering of time. You cannot be truly free if you offend time. When disrespected, time retaliates by suspending your independence—through the unbearable chain of boredom.

Therefore, the lazy person is not so much a prepared human being as he is a missing ingredient in the recipe of others. He is the embodiment of a flavor of life—the bitter taste of non-interest, the very essence of guaranteed failure—something others observe, judge, and feel, only to act thereafter in perfect opposition to the allure of a life spent in idleness. The lazy one becomes a fundamental example, a counter-example, an absolutely necessary figure within a society obsessed with self-affirmation. If he did not exist, to whom would the model of purposelessness attach itself? As stated before, the power of example reigns supreme in community, and the passive man is a specimen of purebred, for he is the finest anti model. And that makes him, paradoxically and without irony, the purest form of a selfless human: one who generates more motivational energy for others than he ever consumes himself. And the most striking part? He doesn't even know. He is unaware simply because he does not care, and others, generally, do not bother to tell him.

When it comes to human speech, one might sense that opinions are subdued by fear—fear of consequence, of reply, of inflicting pain, discomfort, or hatred; and, at the far end of the spectrum, by indifference. Man is so hypocritical in his speech that he feels no shame in addressing God, voicing his pleas, his problems, asking for help, involvement, or an answer—demanding His attention—yet he lacks the courage to say what he thinks to the face of another person.

How can one speak directly to the Creator with personal demands, yet not muster the boldness to begin a conversation with a neighbor? How can one rebuke God without trembling, yet shy away from offering a simple compliment? How is it possible to blame the Divine for human suffering, yet remain silent in the face of a small injustice?

The spoken word is not merely power, it is a dimension that imitates the very fabric of the Universe. To say that the word is power would be imprecise; it mimics power, but it contains far more. The word reflects vibration, intensity, radiation, frequency, gravity; everything that constructs the Universe. Moreover, it reproduces light, or summons darkness; it brings warmth, or casts cold; it offers song, or unleashes noise. Speech is, in essence, the soul that animates human creation. It is the pleasure of realizing potential, the tremor that stirs the inertia of change. It is, fundamentally, everything a human being possesses in the routine of their concern.

Nothing that is lived gains significance without the expansion of thought released through speech. Without mastery over words, the recipe of life is brewed in accordance with deficiency, and the result is a product of pitiful substance, an existential expiration date. To taste any of life's flavors, a person needs, beyond breath, one more element: the ability to refine conversation.

Where breath is an involuntary reflex, speech is a voluntary act—an innate capacity, yes, but one which must be consciously refined. The best advice, the most valuable lesson a person may ever receive, lies in the word: in the importance of mastering, arranging, and expressing it. It is man's foremost priority, his clearest mark of distinction, the proud contribution to his own spectacular becoming.

Nothing acts more forcefully upon the existential experience than an enterprising vocabulary. In every interaction, in every collection of aphorisms, in every philosophical reflection, in every product of thought, there is a syllabic signature, a civilizing process contradictory to wildness. Though imperfect in formation, it emerges from the desperate need to dwell in a space faithful to creation.

Indeed, the word expands the Universe of consciousness through the contemplation of making, through the selective absorption of the outer world. Creativity, in the end, is nothing more than realization through ideas, and these ideas are not a rigid standard imposed by thought, but a profound perspective on how we subordinate ourselves to the exterior, synthesized within the absurdity of a compressed complexity of endless inner revolts. If everything had originated from a place of rational consolation, then nothing would remain grounded in the feeling of conception, and thought expression would shrink to the fragile act of recognition. But because man has the ability to receive information, to merge it with his own voice, and to discard the useless, this leads to a singular existential tool—one that exterminates the dormant primate within the individual's internal liberty, clearing space for the emergence of an exceptional species.

This planet should not have been named Earth—it should have been called *Word*. The great masterpiece of this world does not reside entirely in what can be seen with the eyes; it lies, in partisanship, within the horizon of abstract concepts. What beauty would perception hold without the adornments of love, beauty, faith, freedom, justice, truth, honor, morality, hope, loyalty, peace—and so on?

What would love be if it were not abstract? Likely, a striking emptiness, a vivid dissolution, an incapacity for assimilation. Habits themselves are ideas born from empirical interaction with reality, generating opportunities to deepen understanding beyond the transient experience. In practice and in truth, the ability to think abstractly is a remarkable faculty of the human brain, one that positions man as a unique living being upon this planet.

In daily life, we think more in abstract ideas than in concrete examples, especially after the consolidation of knowledge. For instance, when a parent teaches a child to count on their fingers, there arises a confusion in the child's mind between "number" and "finger," resulting, for a time, in a memory painting, a belief that numbers are names of fingers. Eventually, the child will grasp the abstract notion of counting and erase the association with objects.

The difference between a child and an adult is, paradoxically, their similarity: both engage in the intellectual manipulation of meaning. At every stage of life, meaning is philosophy with boundaries—a form of knowledge without definite answers.

Life is much irony: it begins in infancy with no knowledge and no limits, and ends in old age with vast knowledge and narrow intentions. Man lives gradually through conversion into limitation. As life draws to its close, things begin to lose their vastness and their meaning.

This is what life is truly about: beginning in the darkness of unknowing and rolling the mind through the prominence of objective reality, with the purpose of illuminating the abyss of information, enriching it with faith. Man's purpose is to reach a state of illumination. Toward that he strives, though few have truly neared the target. The common person halts at knowing rudimentary, at best elementary notions, while the others, the radiant ones, are rarely absorbed into inner instruction.

Illumination is not a collective mission of humanity; it is an individual espionage into the information of the Universe. Based on such singular insights, when they are shared, humanity earns its moments of evolutionary revelation.

For this reason, complete knowledge is not an ingredient in the recipe of being human, it is rather a delicacy reserved for those bold enough to pursue the flavor of absolute insight. What matters is knowing that without experiencing objective reality, without awakening the conscience, and without passing through the pitch-black of inner obscurity, no one can transform knowledge into genuine epistemological awakening.

Why is it vital that man pass, even if briefly, through the lowest thresholds of experience? Because it is there that the most powerful revelations are born, and from there he shapes the path of his own life. He does not step onto a road made visible by another. What is essential is the emergence from that dark season, a state ordinary to all lives at some point—but one that cannot be surpassed with borrowed time or artificial light. There is but one way through: forward. In truth, every abyss remains open unless man seals it with his own footprints and the steadfast will to press on.

It is fundamental that knowledge be forged in cohesion with the concrete, for one to live from habit and die from exhaustion. When a person cultivates a form of knowledge mingled with presumption, they end up living by accident and dying from restlessness. Knowledge sculpted by the word in the atelier of reality is the most dissonant instrument for shaping the grotesque. More than that, without even a minimal foundation of knowledge, a human being cannot even qualify as an existential "kitsch"—they are a fracture, a rupture.

There is no other path to the development of consciousness but through direct interaction with, interpretation of, and modeling upon reality. In a laboratory, one might construct a beast, but never an eminent mind. An intellectual proprietor is merely a tenant in reality—he uses the tangible to master the property of meaning, to acquire the wealth of understanding and the asset of the true, to temper the weight of reverie within finitude. And the price he pays, without the possibility of return, is extracted throughout the course of living; it is subtracted from the capital of time.

Naturally, every experience, every introspection, eventually becomes a mere standard within time. Thus, not by closing yourself off, but by examining the external, do you gain the opportunity to detach life from the determinants of deviation. Any path that does not lead to the knowledge of objective reality, or does not begin with it, is a detour, an evasion, a wandering into the courtyard of concept alone.

Within such conditions, within the confines of inner content lost in space and time, deformity is cultivated. Boredom, disgust, and in general, all rejections of the existential offering take root. How could man ever impose himself upon the idea of "love" if he does not first subordinate reality? If he does not test it, it remains a mere concept, never anything real. Through dependence upon the exterior, the inner voids can be filled—as in an unhindered expansion, rich with multiplicity, in a joy so absolute it conspires in favor of one's own legitimacy to live.

He has thought, and he has speech. He feels affection, and

he feels need. He is driven by desire, and by longing. Time pushes him, as does loneliness. And yet, what is man missing to truly live love? Consciousness. The awareness that he lacks courage, trust, and esteem. That he is not fully aware he must fight for ideals, for beauty, for favor. That he lacks the instinct to accelerate the inertia of reason. And essentially, all his will is pampered in the burden of waiting.

Ideals are distant from superficiality and violently lived in reality when knowledge asserts itself as the ultimate sentence against inexperience. The more one practices faith, the more the theory of imbalance aligns with centeredness. And even so, knowledge does not know the unknown; it admits it. What matters is not to take the conclusion as an absolute judgment, but as a transcendence in revelation; a typical form of unlocking the mysterious.

The complexity of knowledge remains fragmented in the realm of empirical experience because it demands to be infused with certain mystical encounters. No one has ever known the complete explanatory essence of nature, just as no one has ever fully disarmed the unknown in thought. Perhaps without mysticism one can coexist with absolute materialism, and without concreteness one can live in complete meditation— but surely, through the absence of consciousness, one dies in the routine of nothingness. The most undeniable and simplest recipe for unspoiled living is balance of ingredients.

Still, it is never out of the question that the vitality of knowledge be harmed by flawed questions and counterfeit answers, or by unfortunate answers to optimistic questions, or why not, by answers without questions, and questions without answers.

Faith is the only abstract concept that contradicts universal confusion. It blends all dramatic perceptions into a favorable vision, attributes absolute truth to existence, and adds harmony to all that depends on consciousness. Why reject faith when it brings meaning to the inexplicable and agreement to thought? Faith spontaneously seasons life's recipe with peace and joy. And the other flavors are also shaped by the act of Providence.

This is what atheists will never understand: that you don't need to prove something in order to feel it. That what matters is not seeking evidence, but receiving help. That not all that is real can be seen. That all which pertains to beauty comes from the heart.

The very presence of mystery alongside faith proves that it has meaning. If everything were comprehensible, if nothing remained veiled in enigma, reality would no longer be real, it would be immutability. Therefore, to withhold faith because of the absence of proof of God's existence is a critique of reality, not an honor to reason. The primordial foundation of this world is the shrouding in mystery and its unveiling, and had the existence of the Creator been evident, the world would have lost its meaning; reality itself would have unraveled.

Without the unknown and the undiscovered, what bond would remain between life and living? How can one refuse to believe in mystery precisely because it is a mystery, and then call that a profoundly rational position?

Therefore, above all, the priority is to be yourself in any incomprehensible situation—to surrender the notion of the impossible-to-understand to the dignity of faith—and the path will illuminate with the feeling of serenity. Instead of contemplating knowledge and experience, man encloses himself within the mystery of ignorance until he is buried in triviality, because most of what he cannot explain comes from nonexistence. Without the assurance of a mystical explanation in the face of confusion, especially behind the veil of the unknown, no one will reduce absolute ambiguity to conditioned clarity. The condition being, of course, the acceptance that God is not obliged to show He exists, but that man should recognize the glamor that comes through the denial of His nonexistence.

Alignment with wisdom comes through the word of faith, and in its absence, the conscience enters into agreement with the overcomplication of explanation. Indeed, a wise person is not one who needs many words to clarify an enigma; he expresses it simply, understandably, and above all—beautifully. Something the atheist cannot do—he constructs a heavy, convoluted explanation, full of pragmatism, and at times, delivered harshly. The word and the thought, when born of faith and validated through freedom from dependency, not subjected to the doctrine of concrete proof, erase that black stain of confusion that spreads through all branches of existence. And beyond that, it bears the fruit of knowing an absolute loyalty to a more permissible form of living.

Man must be loyal to the moral principles he cannot deconstruct, not for the good of society, but for his own. Why should he self-invite liberation from the freedom of ethics, when through the conscience awakened by trust in the divine, he becomes open to any validation and justification of a worthy motive found within the constraints of guided contradiction? For it is through thought, and later through word—mystically consolidated—that one renounces imprisonment in incongruence and accepts absolute truth as the answer to the question of recognizing a world cloaked in mystery.

It is not the word that betrays man, it is man who betrays

the word. It is not man who conceives thought, but thought that conceives man. Man is a being who simulates being lost, because no one is truly lost; all who are astray are simply disappointed by their own interpretation. This world is far too small, too simple, too banal for one to truly get lost in it. Deviation is only possible through stubborn stillness, through digging into the abyss of thought; by refusing to wander and explore the world outside.

The recipe for life must be approached from a confident, anti-negationist perspective, not excessively optimistic, nor pessimistic, and even more so, with no place for falsehood as a means of salvation. The central element of the preparation, the defining virtue of human nature, the solution offered at the edge of knowledge's condition, everything that exists and endures in a life resolved through the understanding of the external world, rests on a single universal concept: *the word*.

Concretely, no one can hold firm convictions about existence and human identity without first mastering the art of conception. If life does not assert itself through the autonomy of ideas, whether borrowed or self-generated, then the only thing left is to witness the unraveling of coherent connections with the offer of lived experience, and the ability to recognize and understand reality, transposed into mental doctrine, becomes impaired. Without a command of abstraction, the individual becomes an unskilled observer of the external world, a stranger to the objective gradation of action, for he will be capable only of absorbing the measure of what matters least: the spirit of nothingness.

Let this not be confused with foolishness, for the inept understand reality, but narrow it within the limits of ignorance. Were it otherwise, the wise would have naturally distanced themselves from the deformity of existence—easily, intuitively, self-evidently. But that is not the case.

To feel life as an unbearable burden is a phenomenon distinct from merely believing in baneful. It is self-evident that each harmful detail should not be countered with even more knowledge; rather, the more effective method is to fight for one's own conviction. The battle against ideological suppression has little to do with a graduated vision between foolishness and intelligence; it is, more precisely, a blind glorification of a dialect formed in the tension between the ideal and reality.

Stupidity is when words are chosen; intelligence lies in chosen words. These are not the same. The intelligent person has the ability to select what he says and thinks, while the inept has only the reflex to use what is already stated, which means that the intelligent is limited by preference, while the fool is limited by available options.

This explains why, in many situations, especially common ones, the intelligent fall more easily into the trap of missing the significance of seemingly trivial details. Consequently, they filter only for importance and blend into deformity. Meanwhile, the inept, through a convenient self-irony, prepares and cooks a life's flavor much more elegantly shaped by ugliness, and in the same tone, one in harmony with imperfection.

Both can suffer from "life dysmorphia", because it is a matter of ideal versus real, but one leans forcefully toward idealism or realism, while the other doesn't know which behavioral notion to adopt. Therefore, the intelligent and the foolish are two different mental states, opposite in direction, and both represent extremes in understanding the world.

In order not to be contaminated by deformity, the recipe for life must be prepared at the temperature of temperance.

This means that the intelligent must pretend more often not to understand, while the inept must pretend more often that they do. It is left to each one's interpretation to judge who plays their role better.

All in all, if one seeks perfection in an impure world, they miss the pleasure of living. And if one hides their imperfection, they miss the very essence of living. Man is an unhappy and confused animal, forced to build a life, led either to suffering or delight, who unveils the enigmas of existence through the power of the word. And more so, from the complexity of thought, he must simplify his own philosophy of life. This is no easy task, for life, in its human condition, is defined as a constructive effort to narrow down the ideal within reality and the real within ideality—not with the aim of blending them, which is impossible, but rather of delimiting them, which is attainable.

An unmeasured obsession would be the choice to live in the world of ideals; its counterpart would be the preference for that which exists objectively, independently of consciousness or will. Dedication, a sublime act of human obsession, becomes a process by which ideas are compressed under the pressure of one's own admiration. For in an insolent way, dedication implies the deliberate ignorance of a broader experience of the universe. Yet this is not the true cruelty against individual autonomy. The real cruelty lies in how it dismantles the ties a person has with the general consciousness regarding the value of a thing, an idea, a belief, or a principle. An absolute loyalty to either an ideal or a reality becomes a self-betrayal that honors the imperfection of limitation.

Take, for instance, money—tangible objects that provoke obsession and total devotion, especially where life is perceived strictly in the material's clarity. Satisfaction comes with acquisition, ownership, and especially the gain of consumable goods that feed the hunger of need. But without an understanding of ideals, wealth collapses into a narrow, irreconcilable contradiction for human nature.

To avoid a life trapped in deformity, each person is bound by meaning, acceptance, or purpose to outline a grasp of domains that exist only within the mind. Blinded by the material side, man loses sight of the full expanse of existence. To be obsessed with money is understandable. But the attitude of disinterest and lack of reverence for ideals—such as liberty, love, or happiness—is inexcusable. If one glorifies the material but neglects the conceptual, then that person lives as one incapable of freeing themselves from their own dissolution.

And so, the search for a recipe of life becomes futile when certain flavors are neither appreciated nor understood. If one prepares a dish and pours in too much salt, does it matter what other ingredients follow? No—it will become something difficult to savor. The same holds true for life's recipe: everything must be tempered, measured, and known, or else life prepares a banquet of distortion.

This is not a demonization of materialism, but a highlighting of the need for a proper distribution between the ideal and the concrete. If a person fails to maintain balance, both spiritual and material, they risk falling into a narrowed world, confined to the periphery of existential substance. This, however, does not amount to an absolute error; on the contrary, it might be a viable path for certain types of individuals. The point being emphasized is that one must accept balance—between ideas and objects, between concepts and ideals, between the tangible and the imagined—if one is to cultivate a life enriched by a rare, enchanting, and complete savor. Yet under no condition is anyone obliged to choose such a path.

Likewise, on the opposite end, when someone is not obsessed with materialism but devotes themselves solely to an ideal, the same rule applies.

For example, a life lived in the idealism of freedom is a case in point. Those who treat freedom as the absolute solution to existence, who summon its presence in every narrowing of time, and dilute every other concept for the sake of concentrating on absolute independence, eventually arrive at a bohemian life, severed from the discomfort of attachment: to things, to concepts, to people.

The bohemian distances themselves from order, discipline, aspiration, materialism, dedication, and commitment—indeed, from any abstract idea that dares to impose limits on liberty. And thus, they become loyal to a single domain: that of nonconformity. It is not something to be condemned—nor something to be exalted.

Such a person, even if unknowingly, enrolls themselves into a peace born from rejecting societal models of coexistence and thought. They grow accustomed to living within limitations. And so, the spirit of expanded experience begins to irritate, to unsettle the comfort of indifference. Should they show no interest in relinquishing certain freedoms, then surely the bohemian will end up sacrificing other privileges or opportunities in order to preserve their impassive state.

With such a vision, man begins to neglect many elements of human conduct—especially those standardized within the bounds of community—in order to increase his distance from the details involved in the struggle for achievement. Certainly, sleeping late, at times neglecting personal hygiene, the disorder of one's dwelling, a quarrel with discipline, an aversion to stress, to commitment, or to any social conditioning, may all be seen as affirmations—final touches to an intensified state of independence. But if you sacrifice none of your liberties, then you cannot offer yourself up for the sake of identities. The one who sleeps until noon will surely find it difficult to build a family. The one who despises attachment cannot thrive in a relationship. The one estranged from structure cannot coexist with a rigorous vocation.

The examples could go on, but the core insight remains: a life devoted entirely to the supreme ideal of liberty carries with it many deficiencies. The recipe of life is built around a single chosen flavor—yet this narrowing of taste inevitably excludes many other pleasures from the full savor of living. Such a life might remain viable in isolation, somewhere far removed from societal influence, but at the center of a community, it becomes vulnerable to ambient pressure, to the chaos of need, and to every element that challenges nonconformity. Thus, "life dysmorphia" enters a contagious phase. More precisely, no one can remain entirely indifferent or ignorant to what others around them value. When those nearby all take part in a rhythm of necessity, and one feels no attraction to that shared practice, they become increasingly prone to existential dissonance. And that leads us to a fundamental conclusion: even the place where life's recipe is to be prepared must be chosen in harmony with the preferred flavors. In the forest, the aroma of money cannot be savored. In solitude, love does not arrive. In calamity, happiness does not sing. In debauchery, faith does not walk. In oppression, freedom cannot move.

Moving forward, toward the movement capable of penetrating

the conceptual obsession, where man looks, with restraint and hesitation, toward the boundary of escaping full dedication to an ideal. If he devotes himself to that ideal, he remains there for the rest of his life. Thus, we arrive at faith, which may be the greatest hope brought to life—an abstract concept that keeps anyone captive in a convinced present. Convinced of trust in absolute truth. It sounds ideal, and it is, but it can also become a path that interrupts the connection with other flavors, making the recipe of life a preparation steeped in fanaticism and detached from the concrete.

Bigotry is the protection against the fierce criticism of reality. Through his thoughts, the bigot obsessively affirms any response that aligns with divine will in response to any need-born question. Concrete reality bombards man with tempting desires, irritates his hunger for peace, shakes his collection of resources, and despite his stillness, spreads before him the spectrum of experience. What remains for the bigot to do in such a situation, other than to reject material need through spiritual will? All that is left is to thank divinity for his indifference toward the tangible.

It may sound strange, but it is not. It takes monumental ambition to resist the influence of the material world, and not only that, but also a pronounced stubbornness, and beyond that, a voluntary submission to the greatness of creation. Any deviation from the norm, from strict adherence to dogma, whatever that may be, requires reconciliation with oneself after a battle against personal conviction. For what war symbolizes change more than the one fought against one's own will?

The stronger a man desires change, the more he must renounce his opinions, for transformation corresponds to contrariety, while continuity aligns with consensus. If plans were made based on opinions and not on rejection and contradiction, then the only victory would belong to bias. Thus, the bigot remains entrenched in a life dedicated to faith as long as he does not wrestle with his opinions, and no trace of refusal enters his convictions, making his lifestyle one favored by intransigence.

From here, we, as humans, indirectly deduce that change comes directly from deviation. It's logical, after all, that transformation of any kind cannot follow a rigid line. Therefore, any ideological polarization becomes more costly to abandon, even temporarily, with each additional attachment to personal belief.

A cheap exit from full conceptuality—or, if not that, from partial abstraction—comes only after denouncing one's own ideas. A person is refined through contradiction. And this, although not necessarily in harmony with the laws of nature, reveals that an individual's transformation occurs when their opinions are not rooted in constancy. If one clings to thought by imitating omniscience, refusing to subject their opinion to critique, they are unfit for transformation. But if they contradict themselves too often, unable to follow an idea through, they lack coherence.

The theme of change in the context of bigotry arises for a simple reason: because, arguably, faith is the most absolute ideal in this world—and, at the same time, the most difficult to renounce. People may give up on love, liberty, truth, or justice—but to abandon religion, to deny it altogether, is perhaps the rarest act of reasoning available to humankind.

The zealot is a concoction distilled from the essence of faith, an essence that typically appears either prematurely, in early youth, and persists for the entirety of one's life, or in old age, offering a solid resistance to the troubles of senescence. Its purpose is to act as a remedy for unwavering living, a life prepared from the beginning free of impurities, absent of sin, indoctrinated in humility, and above all, impervious to misfortune. It does not sound wrong, repulsive, or blameworthy; but if one considers that the world is built upon sin, then such a path seems uncharacteristic of the human species. A life that has never known sin is suspicious of one thing alone: that there is no. No one is infallible; we all draw the sap of our correction from error. That is the human condition—to be destined to live bent beneath the weight of wandering, guilt, or shame.

And the most blessed sin is self-disobedience. From it springs renewal, from the depths of error arises elevation, and most importantly, through it any existential confusion finds its course.

Faith alone is not enough to live untroubled, it is a tool for introspection and acceptance. If it becomes everything, man complicates his life with a permanent renunciation of the logical and rational understanding of the world. A believer offers himself answers; a zealot pacifies his questions. Zealotry is not inherently wrong—it is a misinterpretation. If God had intended man to live solely for faith, then the world would have halted thousands of years ago, and what exists today, both in the tangible and the conceptual, would be nothing more than the hidden secrets of oblivion.

In essence, no discovery can be translated in the language of Religion; it always expresses itself through the wisdom of searching for balance between the hidden and the possible. Divinity intervenes to carry wisdom beyond the boundary where reason ends. It is a mistake to summon it in a convenient manner as a form of absolute loyalty to a sublime reconciliation.

That said, the recipe of life is left profoundly flavorless when the individual conceives existence as an authentic state devoted to a single ideal. For evading experience fractures one's alignment with reality, not by falsely balancing difficulty, but rather by intensifying it through outbursts of disregard. The formula of life reacts to omission; it cooks up a potion of disorientation, distilled within the naivety intimacy of placing everything upon the inconsistent forms of neglect. Disheartenment is never alone—it is always fortified by confusion.

Disorientation arises from hopes incompatible with grounding; only those who live by lofty ideas fall into confusion. Any hope that gains altitude carries with it the responsibility of a fall. There is no use for an idea to reach the sky if it is not feasible on earth—where man walks daily through the ordinary paths of action. For this reason, the empirical dimension of living introduces a saving regression within the vastness of life—an act that pulls the conscience back from slipping into a radical, abstract corruption.

The person who reconciles the mind with an uninterrupted dialogue with unreality ends up silenced when summoned by practice. They are left speechless when reality demands a response to its challenges, yet they cry out in reproach at the elite of illusory politics. Through timid negotiation with truth, or through states muddled by hallucinations, there is still preserved a dimension of interests rooted in the power of perception—where each person negotiates either deep or superficial compromises in order to govern life according to interest.

To live is to take part in a disoriented competition between "with" and "without." Perception is the outcome of a dispute whose form resides in moderation. Nature is rife with rivalry, but contradiction is the mode most compatible with the human condition.

Perhaps through the pathology of antagonism, living in contradiction is not always comfortable—but it is, undeniably, a corrosive analysis that reveals our agreement with nonexistence. Inner rivalry is necessary in order to distance oneself from the disproportion of nullity, to provoke fatality in incapacity, and most ingeniously, to devise provocative escapes from deformity.

At first glance, two existential doctrines emerge: centering in reality and progression in illusion. Therefore, no one escapes the temptation of a personal utopia, and all are absorbed in a politics specific to their own existence—whether aware of it or not. This implies a profound truth: that all people are gradually filled with the inner turmoil of opposing forces. That is life—subject to the condition of contradiction; it is not, by nature, at peace with harmony.

Once one penetrates the notion of strategy, they begin to perceive life differently, they begin to negotiate favorable conventions with time, and most importantly, to pursue their own interests. As immoral as politics may sometimes seem, it remains the only method for shaping progress. For it unfolds in the proximity of observation, reasoning, solution, and action. It demands a visionary approach, fully anchored in the word, in understanding.

Such is the ideal—but nothing is perfect. And at times, when mistreated by corruption, politics itself becomes a vehicle of regression and disaster.

The ability to navigate between opposing ideas, with the aim of directly confronting challenges and discomforts, is essential for instilling meaning into dissension—dissension that ultimately reveals either a rejection or an alignment. Only in politics do friend and foe live symbiotically in everyone. One can never be sure where opportunity or trouble will arise, and for that reason, it is wise to disqualify oneself from the rigidity of intransigence. Flexibility esteems the enthusiasm of transformation, declared within the mechanisms of the self.

However, what is to be interpreted here is not politics as it functions in society, with all its good and bad traits—this is not the matter at hand. Rather, it is about that internal antagonism which enables spiritual, conceptual, or behavioral reform. It, too, is a form of politics, but one not based on dialogue, instead rooted in personal agitation and internal struggle.

It is advisable, where possible, to avoid absolute polarization, because life will present certain moments in which the only form of help comes from the presence of inner rivalry. While anchoring oneself in reality is the proper path, there also emerge situations in which illusion alone offers the only means of overcoming an obstacle. Paradoxically, man existence is not exempt from those small distortions of perception that rescue him from an impasse; hence, total war with unreality is not desirable.

When reality demands too much, illusion offers a modest negotiation. When illusion grows too costly, only reality interjects with favorable luck. If the road to fiction is blocked, then one must either pay the full price—or worse, fall into deformity.

The ability to mediate between opposing interests enriches the kind of understanding that forms the essence of life's recipe.

Reality seduces with passionate fragments—and passion,

without conflictual events, cannot exist. Everything unfolds under the influence of a strategy to alter universality for the sake of giving a particular shape to the interest of inevitably unsettling any truce with the existential struggle. For everything passionate, man must be aware that he is called to fight a battle, one that liberates him from a protocol of collaboration with general understanding, thereby establishing an individual sovereignty.

The oddity of life, an almost imperceptible paradox, is that reality is the same for all; it cannot be objectively distorted. Yet each person adapts individually in order to form an alliance with what is true, while illusion, though different for everyone and shaped subjectively, is accommodated by borrowing general perceptions that bind one to untruth. Why must one be oneself in order to be real, but be like others in order to be false? Is reality a communion between a mode of perception and personal responsibility? Is everything nothing more than the silhouette of ideas?

In the absence of collective conceptual contamination, man would live deeply affected by reality, without pejorative connotation, because his doses of illusion would be insignificant. He would not be capable enough to produce substantial amounts of falsehood on his own. But when living in community, he imports a significant number of perceptions that diminish his ability to comprehend what is truly real, and thus, he becomes vulnerable to the suffering born of imagination.

How many of the illusions in a person's life are self-created, and how many are imported from outside? Clearly, the scales do not balance. The same man would carry a different burden of dreams, hopes, fears, desires, and disappointments if he lived in two separate scenarios: one isolated, and one in union with others. How many would still chase the illusion of success, of wealth, of happiness, of ideology, if they were not spurred on by ambient pressures arising from others' practices? Not very many.

And this is why the struggle to achieve sovereign mentality is so vital, because without it, without a mental mechanism to filter harmful falsehoods, a person cannot properly adapt to the form of reality that is beneficial to him. Even more, he cannot cultivate those constructive illusions that elevate his life—and perhaps the lives of others as well.

The world has transformed, evolved, or been recreated under the heels of those rebels who dared to walk toward an original illusion, personally conceived, leaving behind a reality that became outdated. One can endlessly delude oneself with the desire to acquire a luxury car, a feverish craving that circulates through society—a harmful illusion. Or, one can contemplate the creation of a beneficial illusion for one's own existence: for instance, to reach a goal that allows one to afford what one desires.

Not everything that is pleasing or useful to some is a rule that applies to all. And perhaps more frightening for the world we live in is the idea that once a person releases an illusion into reality—once it becomes concrete—it indirectly condemns many others to suffocating obsessions over that very thing. The first car did not appear naturally; it took root as a chimera in someone's mind, who continued to develop it until it became real. Afterward, those touched by the fascination of the automobile began, in mass, to generate illusions of possession. This is how it has always happened throughout history. One person creates a "unique" Universe, transposes it into books, and unintentionally ignites countless passions for that imagined world. If this is the pattern, it becomes concerning that the number of distractions and illusions born from existing things continues to grow, while the number of those who could reform reality steadily decreases, as they are captured and distracted by what has already been made. If this supposition holds true, it would be possible to construct a formula revealing that humanity may eventually reach a point where further evolution becomes improbable. The world would be enchanted by the vision of a mirrored fence—a genuine collective delusion that filters out progress. People will dwell in a garden of comfort and pleasure, and when they approach the edge, they will look into that mirror and be charmed by what lies within. They will no longer wish to step beyond that pleasurable filter.

Who would want to shatter the illusion of familiar well-being if progress demands the unknown and the uncertain? At that moment, everyone will be caught up in hallucinations beyond the control of shared consciousness, and society will be overseen only by a niche form of objective reality.

If one considers the current social trend of distancing from creation and gravitating toward the tangible, it becomes inevitable that in the future, novelty will no longer emerge from the emanation of human thought, but rather from an artificial source. Decades ago, reality did not offer such an abundance of accessible distractions, which allowed for a surge in progress, given that the desire to change the world was widespread. Certainly, there will always be those who wish to dream of the nonexistent, stirred by curiosity, but their numbers are dwindling as the totality of what already exists continues to grow.

Both on a societal and an individual level, a philosophy

of awareness must be cultivated—a consciousness of that metaphorical fence, present as a mirage—otherwise the world risks becoming confined to irrelevance. Humanity cannot travel indefinitely within a bubble of the known; it cannot endlessly reinvent or recycle the same things, it cannot keep preparing the same recipe. It needs change. It is in human nature to seek the replacement of the old with the new, because the passion for knowledge without the unveiling of the unknown lacks revelation; no phenomenon is more intense or observable than a protected secret.

Pleasure found in comfort leads to routine, repetition, and banality—factors that deepen the cultivation of life lived in distortion. Incoherently, the ugliness of the real becomes recognizable, and the ugliness of illusion reveals itself. Most likely, at first glance, at a first encounter, the perception of the unpleasant is false; but after a series of repetitions, one's sensation of something, anything, can shift from ugly to beautiful. On the other hand, if after a certain number of repetitions the perception of unpleasantness remains unchanged, then, with certainty, it is real.

Thus, all the oddities of interpreting the surrounding world can only be governed through a sound sovereign individual policy, being the only true self-guidance of mentality toward awareness, and it is beneficial both personally and collectively. It is also important to understand that the unusual is not all that uncommon, it should not be feared, and if you ever consider yourself strange, enter politics and you'll see that everyone resembles you.

Each person is unique in their own way, yet remarkably similar to the differences of others. A distinguishing feature can be found in millions; it is not a single trait that makes one unique, but the combination of many. Every individual gathers a multitude of characteristics also present in others, integrates them into their personality, expresses them as they are, but most notably, embodies them in a spectacular attitude that turns their life into a deciphered enigma through the will of an unreadable fate. To create a character of absolute uniqueness is the greatest competition in the world—one versus billions. You must gather many distinctions, especially rare ones, combine them into a multitude of traits, live beyond the success of imitation, and only then may you, with a touch of modesty, claim to be one of a kind.

Every person is admirably decipherable—positively or negatively, directly or indirectly, disingenuously or authentically—which indicates a single, albeit uncomfortable truth: that anyone is worthy of being regarded by others. For if you cannot appreciate every human being, no matter how failed or accomplished they may be, it means that, in truth, you do not respect life, in all its good and evil. You may pity people, but if you despise them, that is an incurable despair.

A person's life is not destined for the health of perfection; it is predestined for the ailment of imperfection. What healing could emerge from recognizing a reproachable flaw, if not the hope of a revival? The dysmorphia of life will persist in the world as long as man lives in agreement with his own disorders—not merely because injustice exists. Injustice flows constantly; it does not mingle in a monopoly of instability—it is a rectilinear chaos that makes us more upright in awareness. No one can truly master another's success, sadness, happiness, freedom, delusion, loss, suffering, or any other state; at most, they can influence them. But everyone can flawlessly govern their own thoughts. No one should behave as though someone else is meant to sell them truth, love, beauty, fulfillment, or any ideal. Rather, each must be aware of the negotiation required to procure the existence they seek. The price of living is set by the value and inflation of thought.

So, in the end—at the conclusion of this battle, after all the clashes and oppositions of thought, in which the primary weapon has been the word—it is time to return to the beginning, to that cry of struggle: "What is life?" Simply, as a final honor to reflect and conclude it once more. Well then, "What is life?"—it is not a question. It is the purest and most sincere answer to the interrogation: "What do you not know?"

Printed in Dunstable, United Kingdom

68232234R00147